GYPSIES OF THE WORLD

Text by
Nebojša Bato Tomašević
and
Rajko Djurić

Photographs by
Dragoljub Zamurović

HENRY HOLT
AND COMPANY

GYPSIES OF

Text: *Nebojša Bato Tomašević and Dr Rajko Djurić*

THE WORLD

Photographs: Dragoljub Zamurović

Design: Miodrag Vartabedijan

A MOTOVUN GROUP BOOK

Originated and developed by
Nebojša Bato Tomašević

Published in the United States by
Henry Holt and Company, Inc., 115 West 18th Street, New York, New York 10011.
Published in Canada by Fitzhenry & Whiteside Limited, 195 Allstate Parkway, Markham, Ontario L3R 4T8.

Library of Congress Catalog Card Number: 88-81909

ISBN 0-8050-0924-8

First American Edition

Translated by:
Una Tomašević

Additional photographs by:
Carlo Innocenti
128; 129; 131–136; 140–149
Robert Harding Picture Library, London
206-212

English language editor:
Madge Phillips

Co-ordinating editor:
Merima Ranković

Production manager:
John S. Clark

Color separation by:
Delo, Ljubljana
Summerfield Press, Florence

Printed and bound in Yugoslavia by:
Delo, Ljubljana

10 9 8 7 6 5 4 3 2 1

ISBN 0-8050-0924-8

TABLE OF CONTENTS

The age-old enemy of the Gypsies — authority — has impeded their progress and hampered their activities for centuries, as illustrated by this early 19th-century watercolor by an unknown artist.

PROLOGUE

I remember how as a child living in Cetinje, the modest, mountain-ringed capital of old Montenegro, I often passed the time, whilst playing truant from school, in warring with Gypsies.
Unlike other parts of Yugoslavia, in which they have had their villages for centuries, not a single Gypsy settlement was or is to be found on the territory of Montenegro. However, Gypsy nomads, called *Gurbeti* in this region, used to make their way across this rugged country in the fall. In groups of about fifty, ragged, wild-looking, with long beards and hair and a multitude of small children milling around the donkeys loaded with cauldrons, pots and pans, long tent-poles and tattered bedding, they moved slowly towards the scattered mountain hamlets around Cetinje. They dared not enter the town itself as the police carefully watched their every move and severely punished any attempt to disobey the ban. We children had been brought up by mothers and grandmothers on stories of the Gypsies' evil deeds, of kidnaped white children, blinded so that they could beg, of roaming at night through grave-yards, of cannibalism, black magic and the evil eye, by which they could make a healthy man fall ill, go mad or die. For us, Gypsies represented the same kind of evil as the Turks had done for our forefathers. In the true spirit of our warrior tradition, by which the enemy had to be repulsed in an organized manner whenever and wherever he appeared, the children from my street developed a strategy for disturbing their progress, attacking from safe, inaccessible points when they least expected us. On some vantage point, some projecting rock on a hillside under which the Gypsies had to pass along a narrow, winding path, we took it in turns to stand guard, armed "to the teeth" with rocks and stones. We awaited their arrival with impatience, piling ammunition up in front of us.

Then we would see the leader of the Gypsy tribe, some twenty yards ahead of the rest. This was always a strong, vigorous young man who inspired confidence in the Gypsies and respect in all others. With the experience of "seasoned" fighters, we would let him pass and then, raising a terrible din, hurl our stones at the followers. Surprised by our attack, they would falter and scatter in alarm, mothers shrieking to their children to take cover behind the pack animals, while the men regrouped behind some rock to await developments.

Their leader would dash back to them within moments and, together with the other Gypsies, start shouting in a tongue we children could not understand – added proof, it seemed to us, that they were the devil's own brood.

Realizing they could not pass us without a few bloodied heads while we were entrenched behind our rock, the leader would reach for his gun and, followed by several Gypsy youths, charge uphill towards us. We would allow them to come quite close, and then let fly with our stones. The leader would then fire a couple of shots in our directon, a serious warning that it was time for us to leave the field to the "better armed enemy", but knowing we could lie in wait again, somewhere else, with maybe more success.

* * *

Half a century later, we were sitting, one evening, around the fire in the home of the parents of my co-author, Rajko Djurić, in a Gypsy village called Medjulužje, some 40 miles from Belgrade. Four generations of his large family were present: his grandparents, mother and father, brother, sisters and their numerous children. Rajko is an exception in having only one child — a son, Branko.

They listened with attention, but not much surprise, to the story of how I fought the Gypsies in Cetinje and what I and my friends believed about them. More surprising for them was to be hearing such things from a *Gadja* — stranger, who was now a friend of their Rajko. But Rajko had left the "ghetto", got a university degree and lived in the city. Maybe the situation was different there now, maybe there had been changes about which they, in the village, knew nothing.

"Here in the village," Rajko's father said, "we are still Gypsies and nothing more. In the graveyard our tombs are in the lowest and farthest corner, in a ditch, just as our houses are in a ghetto, outside the village. Rajko comes to visit us, spends the day with us, walks around and chats with the Gypsies. They've heard about him, that he's become something big, but he hasn't cut himself off as others have done the moment they got on in the world. On the contrary, he's fighting for us, so we can have a better life."

To all this, Rajko answers with a smile: "Yes, it must seem that way to them. But when I became editor of the cultural page of the *Politika* newspaper, a colleague of mine, a member of the Party who had fought in the war, was annoyed by my promotion and publicly announced that he would not be told what to do by any Gypsy!"

There by the fire, I listened until far into the night to Rajko's family talking about their origins, the position of Gypsies in the past and today. I realized that what I heard could apply to Gypsies all over the world: it was a picture of a people connected by the color of their skin, language, customs, and the never-ending struggle with the *Gadja* to survive and continue on their way.

Where to? What made them cross the rugged, inhospitable Montenegro of my youth? Whence did they come, and where were they going?

"We came from Greece, a hundred years ago," said Rajko's grandfather Milan, named after a Serbian king. "We all have Serbian names for the benefit of the Serbs, but among ourselves we use our Gypsy names." Grandpa Milan is a smith, Grandma Javorka, a fortune-teller.

Rajko's great-grandfather and his extended family — his brothers and their families — were nomads. They traveled from place to place, providing services for the peasants. They mended pots and pans, shod horses, helped with seasonal field work and stayed a few days here and a few days there, depending on how long the landowner allowed them to remain on his property.

"My father often recounted," said Grandpa Milan, "how he spent his whole life traveling until he came to this village. He was born somewhere in a Gypsy tent, at the side of the road, as nomads are born. Several families, his among them, reached this place after many years of journeying, and stayed here. This as a gully, no use for agriculture, but it had a spring of fresh water.

For smiths there can be no work without water. For days they waited for someone to come and drive them away with curses and threats, but as nothing happened, they slowly got used to the place and stayed here. Serbia was then in dire need of artisans, so the peasants accepted them.''

Grandpa Milan still works in his smithy, where nothing has changed since he opened it, some fifty years ago. Only there are fewer and fewer horses and he, nearing eighty, is finding it more and more difficult to shoe them. There are few young smiths: today automobile and tractor mechanics are needed more than the blacksmith's trade. Once it used to be the Gypsies' most prestigious job. ''They'd bring the horse, and something to drink, and you'd take a swig from the bottle. It would be warm in the smithy and you'd feel a warmth around the heart. The peasants paid in grain, or bacon, or cloth.''

He also made axes, knives and other tools needed in peasant households. Thus he was respected and never had any trouble with them.

Grandma Javorka, now 74, was born in the ghetto. She learned the art of fortune-telling and magic from her mother. When younger, she used to travel around the region from village to village, but nowadays, restricted by age, she goes only to the neighboring one for some Serbian feast. Knowing the sort of problems Serbian peasant women have with their husbands and children, she can easily ''guess'' their sorrows, tells them what they want to hear, and makes their everyday life a bit brighter. Fortune-telling is something that is practiced only on others, the peasants, whereas sorcery is for the Gypsies themselves. Now she has grown old, Grandma Javorka spends most of her time in the ghetto, practicing magic for her family and the other Gypsies. No charge is made for this, which is part of Gypsy traditions and beliefs.

''If a man is sick, I act upon the sickness,'' says Grandma Javorka. ''If he's unhappy, I work on bringing back his happiness. I make him a talisman — not the kind worn from birth to protect the child from evil spirits, but the other kind, made according to need. The kind of talisman I make, the wing of a bat or suchlike, is placed under the pillow. The bat is a blind creature without eyes, but it sees in the dark, so it can find and return lost happiness. But not everybody can just put a bat-wing under the pillow for it to work. It can be done only by someone who communes with the spirit world — I can do it, but the other Gypsy women in the place can not. You have to be able to put your whole self into it, see what others can not, fall in a trance, utter the right spell. If the words are said in the wrong order, it won't work. These are old Romany words we've had for centuries, brought with us from the faraway country we came from.''

''When Grandma Javorka casts spells for the peasants,'' says Rajko, ''she uses tricks to take them in. The peasant has always been the dupe of the Gypsies' wiles, outwitted by them for centuries. Grandma Javorka used to give them ether to sniff, or some narcotic substance, and the peasants really believed she had supernatural powers. The peasant is naive because he is part of nature; what Grandma Javorka offers him is 'supernatural', something he can't understand.''

Rajko's brother, Ratko, plays the accordion and his father the violin. Together with Ratko's wife, Vera, who sings Gypsy and Serbian songs, they form a popular trio, much in demand in the upland villages of Serbia. When they perform at weddings, the engagement usually lasts three days. On such occasions they take it in turns to snatch an hour's sleep: the peasants want non-stop music during these protracted festivities. ''We have to last out,'' says Vera, ''or we might get beaten up. But it pays: drunken peasants want us to keep playing and are prepared to spend a lot of money on music.''

Rajko's wife, Nada, works in the accounts department of a Belgrade factory. She completed high school and managed to get a job. She says she has no problems at work because of her Gypsy origin. "I'm an insignificant person," she says, "not a threat to anyone. That's why nobody mentions my origin. But I carry it within myself; it is my burden, my heritage, a feeling that I'm marked in some way. For this reason I've set my own limits on how far I can go. I always feel that if I should make a joke, someone may take offense because it comes from *me,* and may use some hurtful expression. I can never laugh aloud or stand out from the crowd in any way, for fear of being hurt. This is probably not a fault of the society we live in, it is in me, it's my Gypsy heritage, as we have only recently started working in offices. Not so long ago the jobs reserved for us in the city were only the worst ones."

Rajko has three sisters: two live in Austria, where one is married to an Austrian citizen, and the other works as a *Gastarbeiter* – foreign "guest worker". The third is married to a Gypsy and lives in the next village. Apart from this first sister, all members of the family are married to Gypsies. Rajko believes it is still too early for Gypsies to marry people of other nationalities because prejudice is still strong. He recounted his own experience when he was a student at the University of Belgrade. He had been going out with a girl for some time, and they were even talking of marriage. "One day I told her about my family, and she was so shocked that we broke up. She said that it didn't make any difference to her personally, but she would never be able to introduce me to her parents or admit to anyone I was a Gypsy."

Branko, his son, is fifteen and goes to high school in Belgrade. He does not yet know how things will develop as regards girls. "For the time being, nobody seems to notice my origins and by the time I start looking around for a girlfriend, nobody will mind, especially as my parents live in the city and are educated. Of my friends, half are Gypsies and half are not. I stand somewhere in the middle."

This story of the Gypsies of the world could begin equally well in my childhood or today, half a century later, in Rajko's family in Medjulužje near Belgrade, or in any Gypsy caravan, in a rickety cart pulled by an underfed pony or a thirsty camel, in a patched tent by the roadside or a shack on the outskirts of a big city, beside the garbage dumps of the consumer society. This story could start equally well in Rajasthan in India, in Iran, in Turkey, Greece or any other European country, in North or South America... For the story of the Gypsies it makes no difference. The dark-skinned representatives of this, until recently nomadic people live in all these countries, known to us non-Gypsies under a variety of names. For their part, they refer to us as *Gadja* – "stranger", which for them is synonymous with "enemy". Everything is permissible in dealings with a *Gadja*: it is not a sin to steal from him or trick him in hundreds of ways, as only a Gypsy knows how. In the five centuries since they arrived in central Europe, they have become very adept at that, having had to struggle for survival and devise ways to avoid annihilation. When is this centuries-long hostility between the *Gadja* and the Gypsy to end? Realizing that the time has come to call a truce, both sides are now trying to reach a settlement. For the past ten years a world Gypsy movement has existed: Romani Union. The Secretary General of this movement is my friend and co-author, Rajko Djurić. Speaking about the program of Romani Union, which reflects the aspirations of the emancipated Gypsies in the world, Rajko said: "We want to live under the same conditions as the citizens of our host country, with our children going to school, but preserving our language, tradition and customs. The school curriculum

should ensure this, instead of trying to change and assimilate our children. We want to preserve our identity, and take our place in society according to our worth... We realize that no country will give us what we ask of its own accord, so we Gypsies have to fight for our ideas, have to join forces and work to make Gypsies conscious of their origins without being ashamed of them or suffering the consequences. For too long we have stayed on the outside of society, deprived of the basic human rights. My forefathers, groups of wild nomads, were confronted in Europe by organized states that had the power to repress and destroy them. And once we had set off into the unknown, we had no choice but to keep going, hounded like animals from place to place, from country to country. We had to learn to survive, to use secret codes, signs which we left for each other along the trail, to work and to steal, to cast spells, tell fortunes and beg.''

There followed many more conversations with Rajko, beside the fire in his parents' home, in the Gypsy settlement. The other members of the family also took part in the discussions, but the most vociferous were Grandpa Milan and Grandma Javorka. They liked the idea of a book, and spared no pains in giving us practical advice regarding our proposed travels: ''If you're chased by Gypsy dogs, don't run – put your hands in your pockets and stand still. If you have to sleep with Gypsies, always lie a little away from them; don't let them see you have money; dress in rags like them; never pay them anything in advance...''

We talked about the text and the photographs, about how the illustrated book should look. It turned out that the old people, though illiterate, had their own ideas on the subject.

''Tell them, when you write, that Gypsies die young and that only Grandma and I are still alive.''

Rajko, being the expert, was to write about the past, I about the present. In his geographical-historical survey, he describes the situation in their land of origin at the time when the Gypsies started leaving it, gives the reasons for the exodus, and the directions of their movement. He writes about the places where they stayed on the way when they started spreading out across the globe, the historical conditions in the various countries at the time of their arrival, how they were greeted, and what has happened to them since.

We agreed that for the sake of authenticity it was necessary for us to travel with a photographer to India, where the rivers of Gypsies had their source, and visit as many as possible of the countries in which they now live. We should have to spend time traveling with the nomads, talking to them and observing their celebrations and rituals, customs and everyday life. In this way we would eventually find out, among other things, what is common to them all and how they differ, what they brought to the host country, and what they have assimilated and taken from it – from religion to language. We decided that, with short intervals of rest, we would need about a year to do all this. I was to provide an account of our conversations with the Gypsies and our impressions of our travels, for as a *Gadja* I had fewer preconceived views than Rajko, a Gypsy and a functionary of the Romani Union, who already had well-formed opinions on most questions concerning his people.

Shortly before we left for India, Grandpa Milan said to us: ''If you do find out for certain that India really is our homeland, see whether they will take us Gypsies back, so that we can be all together again and not roam the world any more.''

N. B. T.

The palm is the mirror of destiny. Many of the signs ''visible'' on the palm and human body have been described in ancient Indian manuscripts, especially the Atharva-Veda. *The art of palmistry has become a major source of income for Gypsies outside of their homeland. According to Gypsy interpretation, every man's palm contains lines of destiny, life, happiness, the heart, and signs such as the devil's whip, an apple, star, moon, sun, a circle, triangle, and various letters. The combination of lines and signs comprises the ''book of destiny'' of each individual, which can be read and interpreted by Gypsy fortune-tellers* (Drabarnas). *This picture was given to us by Sundeep Jethany, our guide in Rajasthan.*

12

FROM LEGEND TO FACT

by Dr RAJKO DJURIĆ

An old Gypsy legend tells how and why Gypsies left India: "We were living on the Ganges. And our Chief was a powerful Chief, a man whose voice was heard all over the land and whose judgements were final. The Chief had only one son whose name was Tchen. In the land of the Hind, there ruled then a powerful king whose favourite wife had borne him an only child, a daughter whom he named Gan. After his death, his son Tchen decided to marry Gan — known as his sister, though she was not. The people were divided into two factions and a sorcerer predicted invasion and bad times. One of Skinder's (Alexander's) generals came like a cyclone and killed the King of Hind, devastated and destroyed everything, as the sorcerer had foretold. One of our people went to the victorious general for judgement on the matter of a brother marrying a sister. The general hit the man on the head. That very moment the great general and his horse burst and crumbled like an earthen vessel shattered upon a rock. The wind blew into the desert the remains of what had once been a great warrior.

"Two factions arose among our people. Those who opposed Tchen drove him out of the country. A great sorcerer inflicted a curse on Tchen: 'You shall forever wander over the face of the earth, never sleep twice in the same place, never drink water twice from the same well.'" (Chaman Lal, *Gypsies — Forgotten Children of India*)

Donald Kenrick and Grattan Puxon *(The Destiny of Europe's Gypsies)* quote another old legend:

"We used to have a great king, a Gypsy. He was our prince. He was our king. The Gypsies used to live all together at that time in one place, in one beautiful country. The name of that country was Sind. There was much happiness, much joy there. The name of our chief was Mar Amengo Dep. He had two brothers. The name of one was Romano, the name of the other was Singan. That was good, but then there was a big war there. The Moslems caused the war. They made ashes and dust of the Gypsy country. All the Gypsies fled together from their own land. They began to wander as poor men in other countries, in other lands. At that time the three brothers took their followers and moved off, they marched along many roads. Some went to Arabia, some went to Byzantium, some went to Armenia."

Certain facts emerge from these legends: a war which caused the Gypsies to leave their homeland; the name Tchen, meaning "earring" in Romany, which is still to be found as a Gypsy name; the names Romano and Singan, which appear in many sources as the forefathers of the Rom and Sinti peoples, with Sind as their homeland; the directions, roughly correct, in which the Gypsies are said to have fled.

Apart from these legends, which were retold, with some variations, within their own communities, the Gypsies also had stories intended for

13

Europeans. Instead of India, they most often claimed Egypt to be their homeland, i.e. they purported to be Egyptians, thereby leading many scholars astray in their research. In his book *Die Zigeuner*, published in Leipzig in 1783, Heinrich Moritz Gottlieb Grellman was the first to banish all doubt regarding the Gypsies' origins, proving that they came from India and claiming that their language was closely related to Hindi. His work served as a basis for further, more detailed studies.

Among the notable books published on the subject are A.F. Pott's two-volume work and the studies of the famous linguist Franz Miklosich. The latter aimed to prove the Indian origins of the Gypsies and the precise time of their exodus. Announcing the results of his research, Miklosich concluded that the Romany language must have originated in northwestern India (Kafiristan, Dardistan, Kashmir) and belonged to the group of Dardu languages. The homeland of the Gypsies must therefore be northwestern India, notwithstanding the linguistic and other changes that had occurred in the period between the Gypsies' exodus from India and the time when Miklosich undertook his research (1872–1881).

On the basis of his analysis of the sound system, the most stable linguistic element, Miklosich proved that Romany was much closer to the older than to contemporary Indian languages. This meant that the Gypsies had left this language community long before, at a time when the sound group *st* in old Indian languages had not yet changed into the *ht, th* found later.

Concentrating on the Romany language, Miklosich then tried to reconstruct the migration of the Gypsies and the main directions they took. Gypsies migrated via Kabulistan, Iran and Armenia, whence they reached the Byzantine Empire by way of Phrygia and Laconia. Some groups settled in Arabia, while other, smaller communities, moving through Syria, came to Egypt and Africa.

On the basis of linguistic analysis, it is assumed that the Gypsies spent a considerable period of time in Armenia and, later, in Greece, where they may have stayed several centuries before moving into central Europe.

The Romany language is the only "book" that the Gypsies took with them from India: it represents their collective memory and is a testimony of this people's view of the world, themselves and others. Their language is an "inventory" of the material and spritual culture to which they originally belonged, at the same time containing elements of the cultures of other peoples with whom they came into contact during their long, and as yet insufficiently explored road. Through continuous everyday use, the Romany language survived the passage of time and became the key that unlocks the door to the invisible past. But however valuable a study tool for investigating this people's culture and history, the language itself cannot reveal all that has taken place in the past; additional sources are necessary for historical research.

Indians, as even ancient Arab travelers noted, do not unfortunately pay much attention to the way in which things happen historically. Jawaharlal Nehru, in his book *Discovery of India*, pointed out that, unlike the Greeks, Chinese and Arabs, the Indians were not historians.

In our case it is even more difficult, as Gypsies are not mentioned in any ancient Indian historical or literary source. Though a certain people called Romakah or Romashi is mentioned in the *Mahabharata* and the *Vishnupurana*, there is no evidence connecting it in any way to the Gypsies.

The famous Arabic scholar, Mihael Jan de Goeje (1836–1909), tried to throw more light on the distant past of the Gypsies: he considered that their forefathers were the Jati. In present-day India the Jati, descended from the

Jadavasa mentioned in the *Mahabharata,* form a large peasant caste, also found in Pakistan.

If, however, the epic *Shah-nama* by the Persian poet Firdausi (Ferdowsi) and the facts provided by Hamza of Isfahan are taken as the basis of research, it would seem that the Gypsies are descendants of the Lur people. Some 12,000 Lur musicians came to Persia in AD 420, at the invitation of Shah Bahram V Gorh, son of Yazdegerd I.

If one relies on the legends and some now ascertained facts, it seems necessary to start from the Sind, the region that was once the homeland of the Sinti. Sind is first mentioned in historical sources after the disintegration of the Indian empire, following the end of the Gupti dynasty, in the 7th century. This was the period of the rise of the Arabs, who arrived in present-day Iraq, Iran and central Asia in the 7th and 8th centuries. Their advance eastward ended in 712 with the occupation of Sind.

On becoming ruler of Afghanistan, Mahmud of Ghazni, a great warrior and brilliant general, undertook seventeen campaigns against India and in the period between 1001 and 1027 brought the Punjab and Sind under his rule. His attacks on India ceased only after a defeat in the Rajput region.

Wishing his capital to acquire the splendor of central Asian cities, Mahmud brought a large number of artisans and builders from India. It is most likely that Rom and Sinti people, whose collective memory has retained the name of a region in Persia, Khurasan, came with them.

Northwestern India was also attacked twice by Mahmud of Gorh, Mahmud of Ghazni's successor, in 1191 and 1192. This was followed by Genghis Khan's campaign, compared by most historians with a cyclone or cataclysm, since his hordes devastated central Asia. Many scholars believe that it was at this time that Gypsies left India in much larger numbers than ever before. And finally, there was Tamerlane, who tried to repeat Genghis Khan's exploits. Nehru wrote that the memory of four legendary conquerors – Alexander, Sultan Mahmud, Genghis Khan and Tamerlane – still lives on in India. It seems quite certain that the last three caused mass movements of the Gypsies, and impelled many of them to leave India. Some tribes, however, remained in their homeland under various names.

After leaving India, the Rom, Sinti and Kale tribes, in smaller or larger groups, moved from country to country, stopping for varying periods in each. This was in the nature of their nomadic existence, and of the crafts and jobs which were traditionally theirs. But the wars and conflicts they frequently encountered outside of India obliged them to keep searching for some new refuge or sanctuary. Some of them joined the warring armies, first the Arab and then the Turkish; some were assimilated by other peoples, by choice or by force. This process of assimilation has continued, for various reasons, to the present day. Thus the differences, some of which had already existed in India, increased, multiplied and deepened. But despite all this, the Gypsies have never lost their common characteristics, apparent first and foremost in their way of life, and also in their language and customs, on which the Gypsies' national identity and awareness are founded. This consciousness often fostered their isolation, their separation in ghettos, and persecution.

On the basis of the above, it seems most probable that the ancestors of today's Rom, Sinti and Gitanos peoples originally lived in Sind. But natural conditions and their nomadic way of life compelled them to keep moving. Avoiding the desert areas, they found refuge in the fertile Punjab, Jammu and Kashmir, and from Rajasthan moved to Gujarat or descended south of Delhi, as far as the Deccan plain and even further.

They did not till the soil or herd livestock. Most likely, they performed the most menial jobs or were artisans (mainly smiths) and entertainers

– musicians, singers, dancers, animal trainers, acrobats. They also dabbled in magic and fortune-telling. A part of the caste division laid down by Manu's law, they remained faithful to their traditional occupations and crafts even after leaving India. Even today many still do the same jobs or practice the same crafts. In short, they have remained on the same level of development, retaining their traditional way of life, customs, culture and system of values outside their country of origin.

Wanderers of the World

The past of the Gypsies recalls a story by Nobel prize-winner Ivo Andrić about a young man wandering the world in search of happiness who came upon a dangerous road leading he knew not where. Only, unlike this young man, who cut marks in the bark of trees which he passed, the Gypsies left no visible traces behind them. Through the darkness which veils their paths and movements, certain names and words have come down to us, adopted words which in themselves serve as a kind of signpost. The year in which they came to some towns and regions has been recorded, accompanied occasionally by information on whence they came and where they were bound for.

The presence of Armenian words in all dialects of European Gypsies proves that they reached the Byzantine Empire from Armenia. This most probably happened in the 11th century, when the Seljuks attacked Armenia and triggered a population movement from Armenia into Byzantine Anatolia. Instead of dates, we can cite only words as proof: *archich*, tin; *bov*, stove; *chicat*, forehead; *humer*, yeast; *kochak*, button; *morchi*, skin; *pativ*, honesty. Miklosich was the first to point out the presence of Armenian words in the Romany language. In the early 20th century, the German linguist F. N. Finck systematically studied the dialect of Armenian Gypsies.

The words quoted originate from the eastern Armenian dialect, for it is known that in the period between the 11th and 13th centuries, the Greek language was dominant in the western half of the country. This is further proof that Gypsies came to Armenia from Persia, as are the following words: *ambrol*, pear; *amal*, friend; *bezeh*, sin; *buzni*, goat; *diz*, place; *memeli*, candle; *mom*, tallow; *poshom*, wool; *vosh*, forest; *vurdon*, cart; *zen*, saddle; *zor*, power, might etc.

The Byzantine historian Nichephoros Gregoras recorded that Gypsy acrobats performed in Constantinople as early as 1322. This group had come from Egypt and had toured many countries of the Byzantine Empire. After performing in Constantinople, it went on to Macedonia via Thrace.

A report by Simeon Simeonis about Gypsies on Crete dates from 1322. Further reliable evidence of their presence in Greece is found in the Rules of Xiropotamou monastery on Mt Athos from the year 1325–30, where there is mention of "Anna, the daughter of Limocervulos, married to an Egyptian". At this time Gypsies lived on Corfu, which then belonged to the Anjou family, in Bulgaria (King Ivan Shishman allowed a group of Gypsies to settle near the monastery of Rila), and in parts of the Byzantine Empire which were then under Venice. The occupation of Çimpe near Gallipoli by Ottoman Turkish troops forced Gypsies to seek refuge in regions under Venetian rule, both on the mainland and on the islands.

In the same period they arrived in the still unconquered countries of the Balkan peninsula, in smaller or larger groups. There is a record, dated November 5, 1362, of the presence of Gypsies in Dubrovnik. The Yugoslav ethnologist Djurdjica Petrović believes this to be the earliest record of Gypsies preserved on the territory of present-day Yugoslavia.

Emperor Maximilian I (1459–1519) with his Council. Maximilian, a brilliant man with a talent for literature, was a humanist and did much to promote the arts and science.

Despite this, in 1500 he approved the decision of the State Council from 1497, whereby Gypsies were accused, without any supporting evidence, of spying and treason against the Christian states, and thus condoned the first German law against Gypsies.

The Byzantine satirist Mazaris, author of *Timarion* and *Mazaris' Visit to the Underworld,* and secretary of Emperor Manuel II, has also left us some information about the Gypsies. Describing the ethnic composition of the Peloponnese, he named the seven main nationalities, and among them Egyptians, i.e. Gypsies.

By the time the Turks had conquered the Peloponnese in 1423, having previously occupied Thrace (1365), Bulgaria (1366) and southern Serbia (1389), Gypsies were already to be found in all the Balkan countries. They are thought to have reached Serbia as early as 1348; Moldavia in 1370; Wallachia in 1385. Soon after their arrival in present-day Romania, they became slaves of the landowners, knights and Church: there was even a Gypsy slave-market. They were emancipated only in 1851, after which many moved to Hungary, eastern Europe, the Balkans and even to America.

Toward the end of the 14th and at the beginning of the 15th centuries, Gypsies were established in most countries of central Europe, where the chronicles of some cities mention them. When they came to Hildesheim in 1407, chroniclers referred to them as "Tartars", probably because of their coloring. Seven years later they were recorded in Basel, and in 1415 as being present in Kronstadt (today Braşov, Romania). According to this last source, "Master Emaus from Egypt, with 120 followers, received money and food from the city council..."

In the period between 1417 and 1420, Gypsies appeared in many European cities: Augsburg, Lüneburg, Hamburg, Lübeck, Weimar, Rostock, Magdeburg, Leipzig, Frankfurt, Strassbourg, Zurich, Bern, Châtillon-en-Dombes (Savoy), Brussels... Referred to as "Egyptians" or "Tartars", they arrived in groups of 100 to 300 people (not counting children) with special letters guaranteeing safe passage (a safe-conduct pass supposedly received from King Sigismund is also mentioned). The largest group, numbering some 14,000 persons, arrived in Strassbourg in 1418. According to the chronicler, the Gypsies said they were obliged to roam for seven years and had come from Egypt. Their leader "Count" Michael, was accompanied by about 50 horsemen. His brother, "Count" André, on arriving in Châtillon-en-Dombes, introduced himself as "Count of Little Egypt". In January 1420 he appeared with his followers in Brussels, where the city authorities provided him and his people with food and drink. In March of the same year, this group reached Holland, and in 1421 Mons, Belgium, was visited by both brothers, Michael and André. André got to Bologna with his group in 1422, and in July of the same year, this group went from Forlì to Rome to visit the Pope. According to researchers, this resulted in their having a paper testifying to the blessing of Pope Martin V, but whether it was an authentic document or a forgery has not been ascertained.

Later sources tell of their appearance in Basel, Münster and Regensburg, when another "Count", Ladislas, is mentioned. He is believed to have been in possession of a real letter signed by King Sigismund. The group that reached Spain in 1425 was led by John of Little Egypt and Thomas of Little Egypt.

A source gives the date of their arrival in Paris as August 17, 1427. Unlike the others, this report stated where they had come from and for what purpose. The group in question was not large, and had traveled on horseback from Rome. They introduced themselves as originating from "Egypt", whence they had supposedly been driven out for their Christian beliefs. They had been advised, they said, to visit the Pope, and had received his blessing. However, in order to atone for their sins, they had to wander the world for seven years, never in all that time sleeping on a bed. Towards the end of August, another, much larger group reached Paris, attracting attention by its appearance: the Gypsies were dark-skinned, tattooed, even on the face, and wore large silver earrings. The women told fortunes and this, despite their filthy appearance, drew great numbers of people to come and see them.

The source which mentions their arrival in Konstanz in 1430 states that the people in question are "Gypsies" from "Egypt", which is "near Corfu". This points to "Little Egypt", their settlements in Greece, as the area from which they had come.

The next important sources for the past of the Gypsies are the Chronicle of Saxony by Albert Kranz (1564) and Sebastain Münster's *Cosmographia Universalis* (1588). The latter scholar reported visiting a group of Gypsies in 1544, and noted that the older women foresaw the future and told fortunes, that they had many children, were strange in appearance, etc. He, too, was told that they had a letter of safe passage and had been "condemned" to seven years' roaming.

Records show that in the same century Gypsies appeared in Sweden (1512), Great Britain (1514), Norway (1544) and Finland (1597).

The first to arrive in Spain, in 1425, was a group driven out of France. Chronicles from this period record that Gypsy "counts" were received in the castle of the former military commander and keeper of the seal of Castile, Count Miguel Lucas de Iranso.

Another source, dating from 1447, speaks of "a large group of Egyptians" arriving in Barcelona. The Church was at once antagonistic to them, and in 1449 the Gypsies were ordered to leave the country. As they refused to obey, draconian measures were taken against them. In Philip V's reign, they were even blinded. (Similar measures were taken against them in Portugal.) As early as 1600 a group of "*Ciganos*" was deported from Portugal to Africa, and 29 years later, others were sent to India and Brazil. Gypsies in Scotland suffered a similar fate in 1655, when a group was dispatched to Barbados. Another group was deported to Virginia in 1715. France was to adopt the same policy with some of its Gypsies: one group was sent to Martinique in 1724, and another to Louisiana in 1750. The Spanish also deported Gypsies, mostly to their colonies in Latin America, but in 1783, Charles III signed an ordinance abolishing laws relating to their banishment and punishment.

The era of persecution dates, in fact, from around 1500, though some instances are recorded even earlier (in Lucerne, for example, in 1417).

How did this second, tragic, period in the past of the Gypsies begin? What caused them to become a persecuted race which, like the Jews, was supposed, according to the Nazi plan, to vanish from the face of the earth?

The prejudices against Gypsies are not of recent date. Indeed, many have their roots in the distant past and historical events. During their great wars of conquest in the 11th century, the Seljuk Turks overran vast areas, from Persia to Asia Minor, in which there was undoubtedly a sizable Gypsy population. A certain number of Gypsies who were not converted to Islam moved westward before the Seljuks, and later the Ottoman forces. Others, the so-called Turkish Gypsies, above all the Arlije, joined the Turks and adopted Islam.

The age of the Crusades, fought between the 11th and 13th centuries, coincided with the period when the Gypsies were approaching Europe. In appearance, clothes, way of life, beliefs and customs, they were very different from Europeans. In certain countries, Germany for example, they were at first identified with the Tartars, who had swept through Silesia in 1241, remaining in the memory of the people by their acts of cruelty. Certain chroniclers, such as Albert Kranz, made no distinction between Turks and Tartars, or Gypsies and Tartars. The Turkish threat looming over central Europe led to the Gypsies being accused as "Turkish spies". In order to rid the country of foreigners who differed in almost every way from the local populace, the authorities revived the legend according to which the Gypsies had cast the nails used to crucify Jesus! This legend was reinforced by many tales calculated to incite prejudice. From the Christians' point of view, the Gypsies were "heathens"; since they dabbled in fortune-telling, witchcraft and magic, they were branded as the devil's agents. Moreover, their very appearance determined their place in a world divided according to color: white, representing good, and black — evil.

At this time the Catholic Church had already formed an institution for the questioning, torture and punishment of heretics. The Inquisition operated during the Middle Ages in all countries of western Europe. The Spanish Inquisition, the most feared of all, was established in 1480 and abolished only in 1834. Heinrich von Wislocki states that in some countries Gypsies were persecuted and punished as heretics even in the 19th century.

While Europeans regarded "private property" as sacrosanct, Gypsies did not even have the verb "to possess" in their language. These were two diametrically opposed attitudes, two incompatible ways of life. Living in misery and squalor, Gypsies were obliged to steal and rob in order to survive, and to this day they have remained "thieves" in the eyes of most people. If we add to this the fear of travelers bringing sickness, especially the plague, which in the 14th century alone killed 25 million people in Europe, and also their language, unintelligible to the Europeans, which was for this reason often adopted by criminals, then it becomes clear why the Gypsies' journey through Europe was marked over the centuries by several hundred laws and regulations designed for their persecution, culminating in the Second World War in the crematoria, in which more than half a million Gypsies met their death.

Gypsy Life

Living for centuries as nomads, the Gypsies preserved many of their ancient customs and beliefs. Regardless of their frequent moves, their life was basically a vegetative way of survival, a passive form of existence that made them susceptible to superstition and slaves of traditional codes.

The feeling of belonging is strong in this society, which is still a union of blood, language and custom. Tribal organization survived longest among the Kalderash people, still predominantly nomads until recently.

The center of this nomadic or semi-nomadic tribal way of life is, first and foremost, the *tsara*, the Gypsy caravan or covered waggon, which is the home of one, two or even more generations. (The Banjara tribe in India call this type of caravan *tanda*.) The number of generations living together is the result of the Gypsies' early marriages. They are bound together by close kinship: as they themselves say, they are "the same blood, the same eyes, the same soul, one belly and one happiness" *(jek rat, jek jakha, jek dji, jek porh, jek baht)*. Life within the caravan is regulated by moral and traditional norms, which also determine the division of work. The men of the Kalderash tribe make pots and other brass objects, while the women tell fortunes. Several *tsaras*, belonging to brothers and their descendants with their families, make up a *vitsa*, derived from the Romanian word for "vine" or "family tree". The *vitsa*, as the Gypsies themselves explain it, represents "the fingers of the same hand", while the great *vitsa (bari vitsa)*, made up of several such communities, is described as "the fingers of both hands". The great *vitsa* usually has one forefather and is frequently named after him on the patrilinear principle. Thus, for example, we find names such as Mineshti, Frunku-leshti, Chukureshti, Belkeshti, Paleshti, Coheshti, among Kalderash groups in Yugoslavia, Romania, Hungary, Poland, Czechoslovakia, France, Canada, the USA and Argentina... This does not necessarily mean that these share the same origins, but the names prove that, in the more or less distant past, they all belonged to the same cultural type.

The joining of two or more great *vitsas* creates a tribal group of up to 100 or more caravans. But such large groups occur only occasionally and are not of long duration, since external social conditions are rarely conducive to this. A group of Gypsies usually satisfies the needs of a certain community, to which they offer their services and wares. If the group is very large, then supply exceeds demand. Moreover, life in such large groups is not as idyllic and harmonious as it may appear to some romantics. A feeling of belonging and of common tradition is not enough by itself to maintain peace and order.

The patrilinear system was likewise the determining factor when Gypsies came to live in settlements, which in the Romany language are also called *tsara*, i.e. caravan. They generally use the verb *beshav* meaning "to stay" rather than "to live" somewhere. Implying as it does a short break, a rest, after which the journey is continued, this clearly reflects the way they lived for centuries. Inhabitants of Gypsy villages usually have the same surnames.

Historical drawing of a Gypsy smith working at the roadside.

Life in settlements differs from that of the travelers: although set apart by tradition, superstition and prejudice, the Gypsy settlements are part of a wider social community. The social and cultural life of settled Gypsies has thus acquired some of the characteristics of the surrounding society, differentiating them from nomads such as the Kalderash.

MARRIAGE AND THE FAMILY. The Romany language has no words for "marriage" and "family". A woman will usually say *lav rom* and a man *lav romni* to mean "I'm getting married", while the expressions *romeste sem* and *si man romni* denote the married state. From this it can be seen that the Gypsies married only among themselves. The practice of endogamy (marrying within the tribe), still widespread today, is part of the Gypsy tradition: marriage with a non-Gypsy used to mean exclusion from the Gypsy community. This custom, though cruel, was a means of self-preservation.

A wife is acquired by purchase, exchange of goods or sometimes, though rarely, by abduction. Since Gypsies marry very young, the marriage contract closely links the families, which are part of a settlement or group, and through them the *vitsas*. The Kalderash, Lovar and some other tribes buy their wives, while the Gurbeti, and Arlije, for example, acquire them by exchange.

The custom of purchasing a wife had a particularly strong influence on the life of the Kalderash and almost isolated them from other Gypsy tribes. The fact that a woman has been bought means that she is regarded as a possession, although rules and norms do not permit her to be treated as a chattel. The Kalderash woman acquires her status first and foremost as a *drabarni*, a sorceress, whereas in other tribes fortune-telling may be a desirable accomplishment but is not the obligatory way of earning a living.

The type of marriage formerly characteristic of the Kalderash is what anthropologists call the "exchange of sisters". Families exchanged brides, which meant that from the financial point of view (expressed in ducats), one received as much as one gave. However, since this kind of physical exchange was not always possible, it was gradually replaced by straightforward purchase. The original ritual exchange of ducats has become a purely commercial transaction. (A bride can cost as much as 100,000 US dollars!)

If both families consider the price of the bride to be right, then the two sets of parents are friends *(hanamika);* if it is considered steep, the bride's parents are "strangers" *(straine)* for the groom and his family.

20

Gypsy tribes have also preserved vestiges of the caste system, which is best illustrated by their understanding of "clean" and "unclean", a factor taken into consideration where marriage is concerned. Marriages are concluded mostly between members of the same tribe, in order to "ensure purity" and "preserve unity".

For the researcher, the words used for family relationships are highly significant, providing as they do an insight into the past social structure of the community, since such names are slow to change. Analysis shows that these Gypsy words are identical or very similar to those in Sanskrit and even contemporary Indian languages: father – *dad;* mother – *dej;* brother – *phral;* sister – *phen;* son – *chavo;* daughter – *chei;* husband – *rom;* wife – *romni.* (The words *mursh,* "man", and *juvli,* "woman", are used only to differentiate between the sexes and not to indicate relationship.) All these are blood relatives except for the last two, whose relationship is established by exchange or purchase. Romany has precise terms for secondary relationships on the father's side, whereas on the mother's they are mostly descriptive (e.g. uncle's wife). Finally, there are the names of the so-called third group denoting relationships between primary and secondary relatives. For some of these there is one word while others are descriptive phrases: for example, *papo* – grandfather, and *mami* – grandmother, compared with *chavesko chav* – grandson, and *chaveske chei* – grandaughter.

Researchers have noted that Gypsies address each other as "brother" and "sister", an expression of their sense of belonging to the same ethnic community.

Family relationships are much stressed, for the strength and status of the group within the tribe are based on them. It is easy to understand why Gypsies express their wish for a "large family" in songs and prayers. Childless marriages are considered a great misfortune and often end in divorce.

AUTHORITY. Within a tribal group authority is usually of a traditional and charismatic character. Its legitimacy rests on the sanctity of age-old rights and customs. (Gypsies say of their tradition that it dates from "when God walked the earth".) But the person in whom power is vested must not only be well acquainted with tradition – *romano chachipe* – he must also possess "charismatic" qualities. Such a person is called *baro manush* –"great man", or *batalo manush* –"happy man", and is the most likely to become the tribal elder.

The elder differs from the others in dress and bearing. The insignia of his authority is a silver cane engraved with the *semno,* a symbol composed of five ritual figures: the *nijako* (part axe, part hammer), the sun, the moon in its first quarter, a star and a cross. The cane ends with a silver apple.

CRAFTS. The Gypsies inherited many occupations and crafts from their ancestors, who learned them in India, Iran and Armenia, lands rich in iron and other ores. Equipped with this knowledge they came to Asia Minor and Europe, where they were smiths, but also woodcarvers, basketmakers, and musicians. At the time of their arrival in the Balkan peninsula, the local population, mostly farmers, disdained the practice of crafts, an attitude which was advantageous to Gypsy artisans, especially smiths. However, as the needs of the population at that time were limited, the groups of smiths had to split up and settle in different villages and towns. This was also the case with other types of craftsmen. In consequence, certain groups eventually forgot the Romany language and partially lost their other ethnic characteristics as they started mixing with other sections of the population. Among the first to settle in this way were the Tamar, a group of Gypsy smiths. This process did not bypass the other Gypsy groups and gave rise to differences among them

A group of musicians with a violin, cello, zither and flute. Probably from the Balkans.

– in color of skin and general physical appearance, in dress, beliefs, and their language – the Gypsies' "sole birthright".

The earliest record of Gypsy smiths dates from 1496, but already from the 16th century on, they are mentioned in many countries. They were also very useful for the armies, making and repairing weapons, shoeing horses, and supplying ammunition, as they knew how to make saltpeter and gunpowder. They are likewise mentioned in various sources as shipbuilders, woodcarvers, miners, goldpanners, ostlers, healers, fortune-tellers and seers, bear-tamers, acrobats and beggars, and in old travel books mostly as musicians, singers and dancers. All these professions are still practiced by Gypsies, in India as well as among groups in Europe, America and Africa. Certain groups were named after their craft, such as Aurari (goldpanners) and Ursari (bear-tamers).

All these were traditional Gypsy occupations, or menial jobs which the local population disdained and which the Gypsies had to accept in order to survive. As with certain other old peoples and tribes, Gypsies work only in order to provide for the "needs of the moment". In other words, they do not have the attitude to time which gives existence a historical perspective and which is conducive to work as an existential practice. Since the Gypsy view of existence is still essentially pre-historic, they live in much the same way wherever they are – in the Balkans, West Germany, France, the USA or the Soviet Union.

Naturally, they must make concessions to their broader social environment, which has always been their source of life: that is where they obtain food and clothing, find raw materials, sell their wares or offer their services. From a very early age, Gypsies are obliged to learn the language of the milieu and the rules which govern it. They have learned from experience, that they must use wiles to survive.

"If you want to survive, you must be a devil!" says one Gypsy proverb. Another rule is: "You are a Gypsy, and a Gadja is a Gadja." And finally there is the warning: "Gypsies drown in the shallows." These three sayings sum up the code of Gypsy behavior in society – everything else, in their view, is predetermined by fate.

Customs and Traditions

The word "custom" does not exist in the Romany language: all the forms and codes of behavior which are traditionally handed down they explain by: "Our ancestors did so, and so do we. This is how it should be." Nevertheless, customs follow Gypsies from the cradle to the grave. When a child is born, it is "introduced" to the world after the umbilical cord has been cut. First of all a red cap is placed on its head, then red wool is tied around its arms and lastly a red amulet is given. All this is done to ensure a happy childhood. After the seventh day, the Fates (Urme) determine the child's destiny, and the mother must not sleep that night, "so that the child's luck shall not fall asleep". According to tradition, the Fates live at the court of Queen Keshali, who "weaves the shirt of good fortune". Together with the queen, they built the palace of the gigantic bird, Charani, which is consumed by fire every 999 years, and then rises again from its ashes, like the Phoenix.

According to custom, the new-born infant should first suckle the right breast. In Gypsy tradition, the right side is "the good side", the lucky, true side, as its name chachi rig implies. Numerous customs follow the child's life until puberty, when it is initiated by many rituals into the world of adults. The traditional Gypsy mariage has been preserved to this day among the Kalderash and Lovar. In this ceremony, the groom kneels on his left knee, the bride on her right, face to face. The bestman places pieces of bread on the couple's knees, and pours salt on them. The groom takes the bread from the bride's knee with his mouth, and she from his. While they eat the bread, the bestman chants: "Good fortune and happiness be with you. And even if salt and bread become enemies, may you live in happiness and harmony."

Finally, there are the funeral customs, derived from various beliefs and superstitions. The actual burial rites are usually those of the faith to which the Gypsy belonged (Islam, Catholicism, Protestantism...), but in addition there are observances connected with Gypsy beliefs, one of the strongest being the belief in vampires.

Notable among the many customs and traditions are the festivities connected with Bibijaka or Black Sarah, who both have their origin in the Indian goddess, Durga. They are celebrated only by some tribes (Gurbeti, Kalderash, Kales); Moslem Gypsies have completely forgotten this deity. Black Sarah is celebrated in May, when pilgrims from all over the world come to Stes Maries de la Mer in the south of France and Black Sarah is carried out from the waves.

Bibijaka (Bibiaca) is thought to be a divinity who lives in forests and on high mountains, is taller than ordinary mortals and shines as though of gold. She flies through the night unseen, enters houses and carts, and shows herself only to a chosen few honest people. She is supposed to be rich and beautiful, and never speaks, eats or drinks. When there is sickness, she appears and carries off the weak. But if a Gypsy cuts off and eats the ear of a dog, cat or pig, she cannot touch him. Bibijaka is honoured in March by a feast around some fruit-tree, most often a pear, which is then named Bibi, after the goddess. Before the celebration, the tree is decorated with flowers and red ribbons, and on the day itself, food eaten on fast days (fish, rice, beans, etc.) and alcoholic drinks are laid out on the ground around it. The celebration starts with the lighting of candles and chanting of prayers ("For Bibijaka's health and Gypsy happiness!"). Then the master of ceremonies – a new one each year – serves the men, women and children with food and drink. They bless him, and he returns their blessing. After this, the people go home to continue celebrating until the evening, when they all gather for dinner at the home of the master of ceremonies.

One of the main Gypsy feasts is St. George's Day, May 6, celebrated even by Turkish Gypsies, who have adopted the Moslem faith, feasts and customs. Until the day itself, Gypsies do not eat lamb, since it is believed that by doing so before St. George's Day, one is actually eating the flesh of one's dead children. The lamb is slaughtered before sunrise. After the head of the family has given thanks to God for having preserved them during the winter, the lamb is turned towards the sun and offered water, so that it will forgive the sin of slaughtering it. When this has been done, the host smears blood on the forehead of each member of the household, the skin is used to sweep the house, and the carcass of the lamb is decorated with willow twigs. The Gypsies believe that the liver of a lamb slaughtered on St. George's Day has magical powers.

The notion of luck is central to Gypsy culture. Despite their adoption of the religion of the country they live in, Gypsies have largely remained faithful to magic, which they divide into *bahtali* and *bibahtali*, corresponding to "white" and "black". Depending on what one wishes to obtain by it, various means are employed, their role and meaning defined by the magic system.

The entire system of customs and beliefs is imbued with the Gypsies' concept of clean and unclean *(uzo – marime)*. The two form an invisible thread dividing life and death, on the one hand, and the worlds of Gypsies and non-Gypsies on the other. The word *marime* (the root is the word *mar* – to kill, to strike) signifies the pollution and decay of death. It is closely connected to the Gypsies' view of nature and the universe, of people and animals.

KRIS. The word, in itself, means "justice", not only in the human, but also in the divine sense, as illustrated by the Gypsy saying: "May *kris* kill me!" *(Te marel man o kris)*. The same word is also used for the institution which is responsible for the settlement of various disputes, from minor disagreements to cases that would come under European criminal law. (In India this is called *panchayat*, the council of five.) The word *kris* is believed to originate from the Greek, although it is also encountered in many other areas, even in Indonesia, where it is the name of a type of sword.

A judge, who cannot be related to either party, is responsible for the correct procedure and decides which of the customary laws shall be applied. A group of impartial observers forms a kind of jury. Should there be a dispute between two tribal groups or persons from different tribes, this is discussed and settled by the elder and tribal council of a third group. The judge of "tribal honour" is greatly respected and often becomes a legend and model for others.

The judge and jury also take into account the opinions of individuals from the audience, who take this opportunity to practice and display their oratorical skill in the hope of being chosen as future judges and elders. The reasons for the disputes are most commonly fights, unfair division of profits, insults and other conflicts and problems of everyday life, even divorces. These are not frequent, but are a complicated and delicate matter since the Kalderash and Lovar buy their wives and the *kris* must then decide whether the wife's family is to return the whole sum received or just a part of it.

Cases of serious wounding, rape, and homicide, grave violations of "Gypsy truth" and tradition, are categorized as sin *(bezeh)*. In keeping with this view, the death penalty was never pronounced as that would itself be a sinful act (besides which, the Gypsies have a strong belief in ghosts); the harshest penalty was banishment from the tribe. Today this step is not taken, as it would have practically no point.

Mysterious Names

The origin of the name *Rom* (pl. *Roma*) – by which many European Gypsies call themselves – has not yet been completely clarified. The most distinguished 19th-century scholars of the origins and language of Gypsies, A. F. Pott and Franz Miklosich, believed the name to come from *doma, domba,* the lowest caste in India, made up of musicians and singers.

More recently, hypotheses of the Rajput origins of Gypsies have appeared. Accordingly, Jan Kochanowski, a linguist from Paris, and W. R. Rishi of Chandigarh (Punjab), have attempted to connect the name Rom to Rama, the legendary hero of the *Mahabharata* and the *Ramayana*, a view which Pott rejected in his book.

The name Rom is unknown among Gypsies in Iran, while the Armenian Gypsies call themselves Lom. Two other names are also in use: *Kalo* (pl. *Kale*), among the Spanish Gypsies, and *Sinto* (pl. *Sinti*), among the German and Italian.

Unlike Rom, which also means "man" and "husband", the origin of the latter two are clear. *Kalo,* in Romany as well as in Indian languages, means "black". (This word, or rather its Turkish equivalent *kara,* was used by A. F.

Pott to explain the name Karachi – as Gypsies are called in Iran. In the Kurdish language the name has acquired a modified meaning –"fortune-teller" or "musician".) *Sinti* also means "men" or "people", and comes from Sind or Sindhi, the region (now in Pakistan) where the ancestors of today's Italian and German Gypsies once lived. Sinti are also found in smaller numbers in some other European countries.

Researchers also cite some 60 tribal names, of which we will mention only those referred to in this book: Banjara, Gaduliya Lohar and Nathi in India; the Lur mentioned in Ferdowsi's *Shah-nama*; and the Gorbati (Gurbeti), Arlije, Lovar, Tamar, Gopt and Kalderash tribes. Onomastic research has revealed that Lovar, Tamar and Gopt are of Indian origin. Lovar derives from the name Lohar and the word *loha*, which in Sanskrit means "metal" or "iron". Tamar probably derives from *tamra*, the Sanskrit word for "iron", while Gopt is similar to *go-pa*, a herd of cows, or herder, and denotes people who belong to the mixed paras caste.

The name Gurbet, found from Afghanistan to the Balkan peninsula, whence it spread to western European countries, is thought to come from Arabic. (*Garib* means "foreign" and the noun –"foreigner" or "stranger".) While discussing names, it should be mentioned that the Banjaras, the largest Gypsy tribe in India, call themselves Ghor, and strangers Kor. The Ghor are followers of Durga (the Black Virgin), also celebrated by the Gurbeti. (A people called Ghoraka is also mentioned in the *Mahabharata*.)

The name of the second largest tribe, Kalderash, is of Romanian origin and derives from *caldarar*, pot-maker, i.e. *caldare*, pot. This tribe, whose members are to be found all over Europe and even as far as the USA, Argentina and Brazil, has best preserved the Romany language and tradition. They are sometimes called Niamcura by other tribes, probably because they

used to live in the Romanian Trgu Niamcu region. The name Arlije derives from the Turkish *yerli,* meaning "local", and in its nominal use "local inhabitant". As the Arlije lived mostly in countries under Turkish rule, they are largely Moslem.

The names *Das* (pl. *Dasa*) and *Gadja* (or *Gadzo,* pl. *Gadje*) are used to denote non-Gypsies. Das was used by Aryans to refer to the indigenous Indian population, the Dravidians, whereas Gadja is thought by some to come from the Sanskrit noun *goccha,* family, or the adverb *garhya,* home, while others connect it with Mahmud of Ghazni–Gorh, the 11th-century Arab general who invaded India.

The names under which the Gypsies are officially known are no less mysterious. In the Arab world they are called *el Nury* (pl. *el Nauar);* in Turkey, the Balkans and the rest of Europe (excepting English- and Spanish-speaking areas), *Cigani* or variants of this; in the British Isles they are Gypsies, and in Spain, *Gitanos.*

As regards the first, some believe that *el Nury* comes from Luri, the meaning of which in Nafasi's famous dictionary is given as: "Gypsy, Gypsy tribe... name of group which is called Kauli." Others believe it may derive from the Arab word *nwr* (nur), meaning "light", since the Gypsies used phosphorescent material when performing magic.

The second, and most widespread name for Gypsies, *Cigani,* has been variously interpreted, but most scholars believe it to originate from the name of a gnostic sect, Atsigani, or Athiganoi, which once existed in Phrygia. The founder of this sect was thought to be Simon, a view supported by a quotation from the Acts of the Apostles, chapter 8, 9–11:

"But there was a certain man, called Simon, which beforetime in the same city used sorcery, and bewitched the people of Samaria, giving out that he himself was some great one:

"To whom they all have heed, from the least to the greatest, saying, This man is the great power of God.

"And to him they had regard, because that of long time he had bewitched them with sorceries." (King James' Bible)

Many believe that the Gypsies came into contact with members of this sect, as they themselves used sorcery. Gypsies are mentioned as *Adsinkani* in a Life of St. George written in Iviron monasty on Mt Athos (Greece) in about 1068. It is from this first officially recorded name for them that most other names commonly used today are derived: Cigani (Slav), Zingari (Italian), Tsiganes (French), Zigeuner (German), Çingeneler (Turkish), etc. as well as the Latin Cingarus.

The English name Gypsies (and the similar Jedjupi in old Dubrovnik, Djupci in eastern Serbia, Jevg and Medjup in Albania) and Spanish Gitanos actually mean "Egyptians", and derived from the mistaken belief that this people came from Egypt.

An Italian, Nicolo Frascobaldi, in an account of his visit in 1384 to Modon (today Methoni, Greece), a port in the Peloponnese, wrote that besides Jews and Greeks, "Egyptians" (i.e. Gypsies) also lived there, in some two hundred little houses and huts on a hill called "Little Egypt". He also stated that they claimed to be penitents and pilgrims, thereby hoping to win the sympathy of the local people. This is very significant, since the Gypsies, on arriving in central Europe, almost always claimed to be from "Little Egypt", and their leaders were "Counts" of Egypt.

It should be noted, however, that all these names are of foreign origin and do not exist in the Romany language.

PERSONAL NAMES. Gypsies almost always adopted personal names belonging to the ethnic and cultural environment in which they stayed or settled. When they moved elsewhere, or when local conditions altered, as in the Balkan countries after the departure of the Turks, the Gypsies changed their names accordingly. But alongside the "official" ones, they also preserved some of their traditional Indian names, such as: Angar, Bhuva, Jano, Hoha, Huta, Hanro, Mandori, Mina and Mujula for men, and women's names such as: Kali, Karika, Kopana, Koiche, Putrika, Turda, etc. These, and some others, have survived to the present day.

To return to the name Rom, used for this people as a whole, it seems clear that it bears a semantic similarity to the names of certain other ancient peoples and tribes. The American anthropologist, Ruth Benedict, noted that the names by which such tribes call themselves are usually simply words meaning "people" or "human beings" *(Patterns of Culture)*. A similar opinion was expressed by Franz Boas *(The Mind of Primitive Man)*.

The diversity of Gypsy tribe and group names, some derived from crafts and professions, reflects in miniature the complexity of India, where 2,378 castes and tribes were recorded in 1901, with the Banjaras, for example, appearing under 27 different designations. Tribal name imply tribal divisions and a social order still based on ties of blood, still fragmented and on a low level of development. Gypsies will be able to achieve higher forms of collective identification only when they free themselves from tribal bonds. This process started among the Gypsies in Europe towards the end of the 1960s. Thanks to the awakening of national consciousness, the Gypsies managed, after many centuries of roaming, to make contact with India, their country of origin, in 1976, when the First Gypsy Culture Festival was held in Chandigarh.

R. Dj.

ON THE GYPSY TRAIL

by NEBOJŠA BATO TOMAŠEVIĆ

India

Estimated number: 35 millions
Main centers: Rajasthan, Punjab,
Maharashtra, Andhra Pradesh
Languages: Tribal languages, Hindi
Religions: Hindu, Moslem, Sikh
Tribal groups: Banjara (30 millions),
Gaduliya Lohar, etc.

The careful preparations for our trip to India lasted several weeks. Zamur bought large quantities of film that he divided into three ice-boxes, one for each of us to carry, then tested the cameras and lenses in order to avoid unpleasant surprises. He even packed a Polaroid which one of us amateurs would use to entertain children and curious bystanders while he took the ''real'' pictures. Rajko packed a bag full of medicaments and disinfectant. Zamur teased him that he would not need any of that as he was only going home, to his country of origin, and would have natural immunity. We acquired sleeping bags so that we could camp near the Gypsies and take photographs of them at dawn, when the light was best, and packed our shabbiest clothes, as Grandpa Milan had advised us. We were quite prepared to descend to the lowest levels of society, on which the Gypsies lived.

Towards the end of February we left for Bombay. We were to be met at the airport by our Indian connection, Ranjit Naik, a Banjara Gypsy friend of Rajko's, who was to act as our guide and interpreter. Without someone who knew the country, language, customs and the tribal elders, it would be impossible to take photographs. Rajko himself, although a Gypsy, would not be able to communicate with his brethren in Romany — their language was very different, probably because those Gypsies who migrated, as Rajko believes, spoke a different Banjara dialect from the majority who remained behind. Moreover, Romany must have undergone changes over the centuries of travel and adaptation. We were even afraid that we might find it difficult to recognize Gypsies in India: their appearance would not stand out in a sea of Indians, as it did in Europe.

When we landed late at night, tired and tense, we looked around for our guide in vain: Ranjit Naik had not turned up. He was to have procured a van for us and we had counted on driving directly to the nearest Gypsy settlement without staying in Bombay. Realizing we could not leave that evening, we spent the next two hours phoning hotels in Bombay — they were either full or nobody answered. Then we called our compatriot, Nada Ahuja, married to a distinguished Indian businessman. She was most efficient: not only did she find us a good hotel within minutes, but came to fetch us and took us to dinner, although it was already 1 a.m. Indian time. As Indian custom demands, the whole of her husband's family came along, some fifteen of them, to show us honor and hospitality.

Despite the comforts of the hotel, we could hardly sleep for worry about Ranjit — without him we might as well turn back. The next day was a Sunday, and as we only had Ranjit's office telephone number, we decided to go sightseeing in this vast city where a large proportion of the twelve million inhabitants seems to sleep in the streets.

The following day, when we finally contacted Ranjit, it turned out that he had not received our telegram. He came to our hotel within the hour: a tall, thin man with curly grey hair and an open, friendly face. The moment he started telling us, in excellent English, about the travel plans he had made, we realized we had found just the right person. He would take us to the areas where the Banjaras lived, the largest Gypsy tribe in India, and we could start the same day by visiting a group of them camped right next to a nuclear power plant. From there we could travel south, towards Puna, Sholapur and Hyderabad. We would thus pass numerous Gypsy villages and camps, especially in the arid Deccan plain, and travel through three states: Maharashtra, Karnataka and Andhra Pradesh, where the largest number of Banjaras was to be found outside of Rajasthan, the Gypsies' original homeland in the north.

However, not everything went according to plan – instead of a van, we found that Ranjit had hired an automobile, a 1939 model Ford produced in India, with a plump driver. He explained that only Indian-made cars could be hired, that it had been exceedingly difficult to get even this one, and no, he couldn't dispense with the driver, as the company only hired its vehicles with a chauffeur. We had no choice but to squeeze in with all our gear. "But how are we to sleep without a van?" Assuming that we wanted to save money, Ranjit answered that there were many rest-houses charging no more than a dollar or two a night, but this information only depressed us further.

After a mere 15 miles the driver stopped and poured large quantities of water into the radiator: this explained the logic of hiring the driver with the vehicle.

Arriving at the nuclear power plant, we saw that the Banjaras had raised their settlement right beside the fence. It was the same kind of encampment that Gypsies build everywhere in the world on the outskirts of large cities: huts of mud and twigs with tin roofs, no windows and one door. As soon as Zamur took out his cameras two soldiers appeared and entered into a heated discussion with Ranjit. In the end we were allowed to photograph the Gypsies, but the soldiers remained with us in case our cameras should stray towards the plant.

Rajko produced the Polaroid, gathered all the children he saw and lined them up as for a school photograph. A few minutes later he was waving the wet print while they clustered around, awaiting a miracle. In the meantime Zamur had disappeared down the nearest narrow alley, snapping away. Deciding to follow him, I wandered down the first alley, entered another and suddenly found myself face to face with a pack of snarling dogs. Remembering Grandpa Milan's instructions, I thrust my hands in my pockets, but obviously not fast enough: they surrounded me and one bit my leg. I dared not run or call out for fear of being torn to pieces, but fortunately some Gypsies emerged from their huts and chased the animals away. Normally I would have rushed to a doctor for rabies jabs, but this did not seem feasible in our present circumstances. I soon found Ranjit talking to the Gypsy elder and, not mentioning the incident, prudently kept close to them for the rest of our visit.

Outside many of the huts old women were sitting – the younger ones were out looking for scrap-iron, waste paper and other refuse that could be utilized or sold. Some of the villagers, we learned, are acrobats, tight-rope walkers, or perform as fakirs in the streets of Bombay.

I told Ranjit of a performance we had seen in the city the previous day by a family – a man, woman and two children who could not have been more than three or four years old. The woman and children, having gone some 50 yards from the man, came toward him turning somersaults. The man then raised a rod from the ground, placed one end against the lower part of the woman's throat, the other against his chest, and started pushing. We watched with horrified fascination as the rod slowly appeared at the back of her neck. The husband took a bow, while the children went round with a bowl, collecting coins. Then they moved to another street. Ranjit agreed that they must have been Banjaras. At first, he said the acrobatics were simple, but when the competition became too tough, the Gypsies started inventing more and more complicated fakir tricks. The hole in the throat is made gradually. It is first only a cut, when the child is young, the wound being prevented from healing by some special salve. Then the wound is gradually deepened, until the hole passes through the neck. They have to know their anatomy, of course, as a mistake could be fatal.

The Gypsy elder, called *Naik* by the Banjaras, told us that the 500 families in the power-plant settlement had come from the Punjab, where they had lived in the wilderness, in a forest far from any city. In 1958 seven families decided to move to Bombay by train, having heard that work could be found there. The Naik thought that the story of a good life and employment in Bombay had been only a fairy-tale, that they had been better off in their own region, but now there was no going back...

There was to be a wedding in ten days' time, he told us. The bride and groom were now being instructed in their duties according to the customs brought from the Punjab. The groom was in this hut, being fed the very best food, so he could found a strong, healthy family. He was thirteen. The bride, in a similar hut some distance away, was eleven years old. Her preparation for marriage was much more demanding: she was being taught to read palms, tell fortunes, memorize the precise words with which to address her husband and parents-in-law, sing and dance. All that she had to learn is called, by the Banjaras, *dhaglo* or *dhavalo.* Having acquired these accomplishments, the bride is bought for money or cattle, and this purchase places her in a dependent position towards her husband and his family. Should her husband die, one of his brothers would take her to wife without further payment. She could refuse him only if another man offered to marry her and pay her late husband's family the sum they had given for her.

We were not permitted to enter the bride's hut and photograph her as she was not allowed to receive men, but we visited the groom, reclining on a straw mat covering the mud floor of his otherwise unfurnished home. Next to him stood dishes with food and drink – after three weeks of feeding up, he was much better filled out than his peers. The Naik told us that the lad himself had no say in choosing his bride: it was the duty of the parents and the Naik himself to see that eligible young people were married at the right time.

We made for the car, where an excited crowd still surrounded Rajko and his magic camera, and piled in once more, delighted that we had started our work. The asphalt road was too narrow for two vehicles to pass – one always had to get off the road into the dust and dirt at the side. The only question was which one. According to our way of thinking, it should be ours, the lighter, smaller vehicle, if there was a truck coming towards us. Our driver, however, was of a different opinion and drove about 30 miles an hour (the maximum our old Ford could manage) straight at any approaching truck, hoping it would give way. The truck drivers, just as stubborn, clearly had no such intention, and it was only by swerving at the last moment that we avoided a collision. Telling our driver to be the wiser and let others pass made no difference whatsoever, so each time we saw a truck approaching, we ducked.

Ranjit was an excellent interlocutor: he spoke of his Banjaras and his efforts for thirty years to improve their status in society. He publishes a monthly magazine called *Roma-Banjara,* which unfortunately has limited influence since most Banjaras are illiterate. He was now engaged on the project of moving the "power-plant" Banjaras to a new settlement being built with the help of the authorities, who had donated the land.

We soon came to a large, straggling Indian village, and stopped near a multitude of tiny shops, only six feet by nine, crammed with goods of all kinds. The owners sat in the middle, crosslegged, while dozens of dogs loitered nearby. Starving cows with sunken sides searched throught the heaps of rubbish for paper or something else edible, shaking their heads and tails to chase away the swarms of flies and the large grey rats creeping around them. We turned from this unpleasant sight only to meet a worse. In the middle of the street lay a dead cow, hindquarters missing, with vultures and dogs tearing out its entrails: everything that dies here is instantly consumed.

This first encounter with an Indian village, such as half a billion people live in, was horrifying, yet strangely exciting. We wandered on. More rubbish heaps, and in the middle of one, a man. He lay dressed only in his Indian hemp trousers, his face covered from the burning sun by a piece of news-paper. He was scarcely alive. A little further away, a dog was dying on a similar heap. The vultures had already gathered, waiting for man and animal to weaken sufficiently for them to have a meal.

Not far off, we came upon half a dozen Gypsy carts belonging to itinerant smiths of the Lohar tribe, who were working over their charcoal fires, fashioning utensils for the villagers. These wares, Rajko commented, are almost identical to those made by the Gypsies for peasants in the Balkans.

When we resumed our journey, we came upon some women balancing copper waterjugs on their heads. Ranjit pointed them out excitedly: "These are also Banjaras! We're now entering their territory." He went on to tell us about them: "Regardless of where they live, they speak the same language. The women wear long skirts with pieces of mirror stitched to them. These once served to frighten wild beasts away, but nowadays they're mostly ornamental. They all wear the same kind of earrings, bell-shaped with tassels, made of aluminium or sometimes even silver. Their metal bracelets, nowa-days plastic ones as well, are a sign they are married. For each year of marriage they add another, so the older they are, the more bracelets they wear. Most Banjaras are officially Hindu, but the basis of their beliefs is pagan. They all share the same customs and traditions. The women wear the same clothes and jewelry whether working or resting, and do not even take them off at night. The men are freer, and wear light clothing like most other Indians, so it is difficult to recognize them without their women.

It was already night when we reached Sholapur. We roamed the dark streets for a long time before finding a "hotel". Next to a rickety table serving as a reception desk lay the staff. In the dim light of a bare bulb we made out more people sleeping on the floor in the hall: guests who were paying less than those in the rooms.

We three Yugoslavs were given a room with six beds in it. After glancing at the bedclothes, we decided to spend the night in our sleeping bags. The cement floor was wet as the washbasin in the corner was blocked and the water overflowed. Cockroaches and other insects crawled all over the walls. "Survival of the fittest," Zamur said, and for the hundredth time we bemoaned the lack of a van.

We could hardly wait for dawn – we woke Ranjit and the driver and – piled into the car, wishing to get out of Sholapur as soon as possible. Though it was still not day, the streets were crowded and we wondered where everyone was heading. Our question was soon answered: in the fields at the

1 This Gypsy leader – Naik, from the Banjara tribe, has set off on his way to Sholapur, a town half-way between Bombay and Hyderabad, as the "vanguard" of the large clan under him. There he will search for a good camp site and maybe arrange for some seasonal work such as cutting cane. Horses are rare in this part of India, so his arrival on horseback is a sign of his privileged position.

32

2   *The duty of every Gypsy woman is to provide two essentials: water and fire. To avoid the blazing heat of the desert, this group of women and children started off long before sunrise on their miles-long walk to the nearest water. The copper water-jugs, called* piri *in the Romany language, adroitly balanced on their heads, are made according to caste division of labor by the men of the tribe. (pp 34-5)*

3   *In the desert of Rajasthan, near the town of Bikaner, we came at dawn across a "desert ship", ready to set sail across the sea of sand. It belongs to a Gypsy family of the Gaduliya Lohar tribe (Gaduliya means "cart", and Lohar, "iron" or "copper"). The men, smiths, have already gone to a nearby village to offer their wares for sale, while the women and children eye us suspiciously. (pp 36-7)*

4   Banjara women must often walk long distances to reach the fields where they do seasonal work. On their heads they carry the food and water they need to sustain them during their long working day, since this is not provided by their employer.

5   Traveling smiths – Gypsies – can be encountered in all parts of Rajasthan. A cart loaded with household goods and possessions, tools, copper and iron dishes, and members of the large family slowly approaches the outskirts of Jaisalmer. Gypsy smiths once knew better times when they made weapons for maharajas and their troops. Nowadays their only source of income is from the sale of metal pots and dishes, which brings in hardly enough to feed the family.

6　An ox-drawn cart going to a fair, which usually lasts seven days. During this time the Gypsy smiths will make their wares and sell them to peasants on the spot, "still warm". When this fair is over, they will go to the next, within a radius of about 60 miles, then to another, and so on till the end of their days. The second woman in the cart, we were told, is the widow of the Gypsy man's brother. According to custom, after the death of her husband, she is taken in by her brother-in-law, becoming his second wife, and her children are also given a place in his family's cart.

7　The smith's cart, gaduliya, is a Gypsy's greatest wealth, and never left unattended. For him it is both a means of transport and a home. These carts, constructed in much the same way since the 16th century, are all partitioned in the traditional manner. The front part has a triangular drawer containing money, gold, jewelry which is not being worn at the moment, and a mirror. There are also compartments for tools, flour and rice. The common bedding is stowed in the middle section of the cart. The whole life of the family takes place in the cart when they are on the move, and under and around it when they are encamped.

8, 9　We encountered this group of Lohar Gypsies in the desert near the Pakistani frontier. Having waited for the men to pass and keeping the engine of our Jeep running just in case, we photographed the ''baggage train'' of the Gypsy tribe. This troop of nomads, numbering about two hundred souls, had been on the move for days. In the blistering heat of the desert they transported all their possessions on donkeys, and led a dozen hounds on leashes. Of the millions of dogs in India, these are among the lucky few that actually have owners. They keep the Gypsies supplied with game. (pp 42-3)

10　After the scorching heat and dust of the lifeless desert sands, this patch of green must seem a Garden of Eden to this Gypsy family. They have left the arid dustbowl behind them and will spend the rainy season encamped in the vicinity of some settlement. In this camp, thiya, they will spend the months of June to September resting, buying draft animals at one of the fairs, and attending weddings.

11　''The wise man carries all his valuables with him''. This Latin proverb certainly applies to the women of the Banjara tribe, who wear all their finery at all times. The design of their bell-shaped earrings has not changed for centuries. Banjara women are easily recognizable by their specific dress and jewelry, identical in all the regions in which they can be met. The ornamental trinkets are made within the tribe from aluminium and sometimes even silver.

12 When the Banjaras settle somewhere temporarily, the first task of each family is to collect thorny branches and weave them into a fence encompassing the area it will be using. Only members of the family may enter this enclave, while the "social life" of the Gypsies is carried on outside these fences. The thorny scrub is also used to feed the fires of smouldering dried dung. This Gypsy woman is preparing a kind of flat bread called roti. Spoons are not used: the Gypsies eat their mostly solid food with their fingers.

14

13   It was not yet light when we came across a group of Gypsy musicians on a hill opposite the 13th-century fortress at Jaisalmer. They had risen early not to miss the arrival of the tourists who come to visit this historic region of Rajasthan. In India the profession of musician is a caste characteristic. Those who belong to it are called barangar, denoting someone who earns his living by amusing others with song and dance. Old chronicles state that, at the time this fortress was being built, Gypsy musicians entertained the Rajputs with their talents. The instruments that greeted our arrival have not changed since those times: they are made of halves of cocoanut shells, sugar cane and donkey-tail hairs. (pp 46-7)

14,   When the rivers of Gypsies started leaving India a thousand years ago, Gypsy musicians were among the first. According to a chronicle from about AD 950, written by an Arab historian, Hamza of Isfahan, the Persian ruler Bahram Gorh asked King Shankal of northern India to send him 12,000 musicians. Enchanted by their music, the Persian king gave them permission to settle in his land. The same story was told half a century later by the Persian chronicler and poet Ferdowsi, author of the Epic of the Kings. Music has remained an integral part of the life of Indian Gypsies, as illustrated by this group we met on our way to Hyderabad.

15   A member of the Lohàr tribe entertaining young people at a fair on the outskirts of Ajmer. With a mimicry in which all expressions and movements are traditional and meaningful to his audience, he represents Hanuman, the monkey-god of ancient Indian mythology. Such one-man theatrical performances frequently last for several hours and, at the end, the entertainer collects coins from those with money to pay for their enjoyment. ''I don't expect much,'' he told us when asked how much he earns. ''In the course of one day I collect just enough to feed myself and my wife and children who wait for me in our tent not far from here.''

16   These two girls are among the fortunate pupils of the school at the Nehru Nagar Banjara Centre. To help the illiterate Banjaras, the government has begun sponsoring schools such as this one, from which some students have already gone on to gain a university education.

15

17

17, 18 Gypsies of the Nathi tribe, renowned as catchers of two of the deadliest types of snakes, vipers and cobras, live near Jaipur. They are known as snake-charmers, but actually belong to a caste of healers, treating people who have had the misfortune to be bitten by a snake. They catch the reptiles during the monsoon period and remove their poison, which they then mix with frog saliva and certain roots to produce a kind of "serum" applied in powder form to the bite. They told us, however, that its effectiveness depends on the kind of bite: if the wound is deep, a man dies in about twenty seconds; if it is shallow, he may live for up to ten days. If the unfortunate finds one of these healers in the first two days, he may be saved.

18

19 Members of the Nathi tribe are noted for their long wooden pipes used for snake-charming. They also carry with them quantities of ready-made "serum" and baskets with snakes which they display at fairs as a sign of their caste and profession. Nowadays snake-charming is performed mostly for the benefit of foreign tourists. (pp 52-3)

20   On the border of Rajasthan towards Punjab we came across a temporary settlement of a clan of the Lohar tribe. A dozen or so mud huts, like swallows' nests, huddle against the blistering sands of the desert. The huts have only doors, and the families sleep on straw mats thrown on the sand. The cluster of dwellings is surrounded by piles of thorny branches, probably to protect the inhabitants against wild beasts or unwelcome visitors, so that the "village" can be entered only through a single opening. Inside we found just a few women, who explained that their husbands had gone to a nearby village to dig wells for the peasants. Rajasthan Gypsies are said to possess a "sixth sense" which enables them to find water, a very precious commodity in this arid land. (pp 54-5)

21   Surprised by our sudden appearance in their village, these Gypsy women hurriedly covered their faces from the sight of unknown men. This spinning-wheel used for cotton seems to date from the time when men first rejected animal hides in favor of cloth, several thousand years ago. The women weave and dye their long, colorful skirts, as well as other cloth for their family's clothing, in the months when they are stationary: June to September. The various bowls and dishes around them contain extracts of plants and roots that give the gay colors beloved by Gypsies. They buy cotton in bales at fairs, or just help themselves from the cotton fields they pass on their long journeys. (pp 56-7)

22 An amazing elegance of dress, posture and movement, in the way colors are combined and jewelry is worn, in the manner of the "Gypsy style" of European fashion houses, comes naturally to women of the Banjara tribe, young and old. Women's clothing and adornment have the function of indicating the wearer's position in the society: whether she is married and for how long, a widow or unmarried. Each bracelet represents one year of marriage, so the older a woman, the more jewelry adorns her arms, giving her a greater degree of elegance.

23 Smiths of the Lohar tribe are not only skillful at shaping hot iron: they are good at making huts from dust and water, ovens for baking bread, chests for wheat and rice, tables and benches and everything else necessary to "furnish" their temporary abode. Such settlements, found all over the Rajasthan desert, often recall groups of open-air sculptures created by some modern artist.

24 Gypsy children come unplanned, and it is natural selection that determines how many and which shall survive to adulthood. A childless marriage, considered shameful and a great misfortune, usually ends in "divorce". On an average, women of the Banjara tribe, to which this mother belongs, bring 10–15 children into the world, but only about five survive. Breasts are a source of nourishment and as such are not hidden from strangers.

25   In the 14th century the Great Moghul
gathered Gypsies from the north of India and
forced them to carry weapons and provisions
for his army during his occupation of the
Deccan plain. In this way Gypsies arrived in
the south of India. In contrast to the nomadic
way of life which they led in the north, here
the Gypsies settled down in villages, tandas,
on infertile land of no use for agriculture in
the vicinity of larger towns. In one such
village, Kokirala Tanda, we spent two days
on our way to Hyderabad.

26   In the vicinity of Kokirala Tanda there is a sugar refinery. The village women do seasonal work, shredding sugar cane by trampling on it and spreading it around with the hands to make it dry faster. Their working day lasts fifteen hours, and is paid five rupees, the equivalent of about 40 US cents. They have to provide their own food and drink, and usually carry the smaller children with them while they work bent over in the dust.

27   With the permission of their overseer, these women stopped for a moment and straightened up so that our photographer could take this shot. It turned out that they work all day long in the heat and dust wearing all their jewelry which, together with the copper anklets, can weigh over ten pounds. (pp 62-3)

33   Fire is a natural symbol of divinity. After a hard day's work, after the cattle and children have been fed at dusk, Gypsy women perform their ritual fire dances. This is a social activity that serves to strengthen the collective spirit. One of the main rituals is connected with Duwali, Holi and Teej. During Holi, an effigy of Lord Khama is burned before dawn, and the Gypsies sing and dance around the fire until sunrise. (p 70)

34   Food is prepared from wheat flour. The mainstay of the Gypsies' diet is roti, a type of bread made of flour and water, patted into a pancake shape between the palms of the hands. The dough is then placed directly on to the dried cow-dung used as fuel. Like most other Indians, Gypsies seldom eat meat, mostly living on bread, rice and vegetables, which are plentiful. (p 71)

35   In addition to jewels, Gypsy women adorn themselves with tattoos, on the nose, forehead, arms and legs, which designate the tribe they belong to. Tattooing is obligatory and is considered by the Gypsies to be the only wealth taken with them into the other world. Among the signs commonly found among Indian Gypsies' tattoos is the swastika. As a result of difficult living conditions and lack of water they do not bother much with hygiene; fairs are one of the few occasions for which they make an extra effort. (p 71)

36   Unlike the women, easily recognizable as Gypsies by their dress and jewelry, the men wear the same clothes as others in India and are thus more difficult to identify. They do little work, leaving the main burden of labor to the women of their tribe. Apart from being mothers, ''housewives'' and fortune-tellers, Gypsy women also do heavy seasonal work, while their husbands spend their time chatting, squatting on their heels in their typical resting pose.

37   Next to the mother and child is the village sorceress, performing rites to protect the child from evil spirits so it can grow up healthy and strong. Because of the high rate of infant mortality, the services of such women are considered indispensable.

38   Even in the greatest heat Gypsy women wear clothes covering them from head to toe, while the men are permitted to cool themselves by stripping off. These women spend hours pounding wheat to have flour for the household.

39

39, 40 *For this Gypsy family, too, cows are venerated animals, providing milk and the dung used for the fire. Cows are not used as draft animals, only oxen. This Gypsy woman standing in front of her hut is among the lucky few to own both cows and oxen, and thus enjoys high status in the settlement. Owners of cattle, however, have an obligation that others do not – each November, all of them leave the villages, tandas, in the region and migrate to richer pastures in the hills. They also hire out their oxen for transport during the season of cane-cutting, cotton-picking, etc.*

41   In Jaipur we came across Gypsies working with elephants. In the past they were the main salt and grain carriers across the vast Indian subcontinent, but this profitable profession came to an end with the arrival of the British and the introduction of railways and steamships. Left without their caste profession, these unfortunate people had to scrape a living somehow, frequently operating outside the law. In 1896, the British Crown proclaimed all Gypsies a Criminal Tribe, and imposed rigorous repressive methods. In this region, however, these tattooed and painted elephants are still the main pack animals. The Gypsies charge for their services by the day. (pp 80-1)

42 Gypsies today use their elephants mostly to transport tourists to the famous fortresses around Jaipur and Jodhpur. It is said that they once helped Alexander the Great to carry back to Greece the treasures he acquired during his military campaigns in India.

43 Gypsies also use their elephants for open-air acrobatic performances, sometimes even getting as far as the Red Fort in New Delhi. Here we see a Gypsy waving colorful cloths, trying to attract the attention of passers-by to his acrobatics. The platform on the elephant's back holds a little chair, on which the performer shows off his prowess, and keeps requisites for juggling. Outside of India, too, elephants are a ''must'' for any circus, and are still handled predominantly by Gypsies.

side of the road we saw hundreds of people going about nature's business, all turned in the same direction.

Ranjit explained that only a few miles further on we were to visit a Gypsy settlement raised in the last few years through the activities of one man. "In India, individuals have always been able to move the masses by their visions and belief that they have been called upon to do something great and good for the people," Ranjit said, probably thinking of his own efforts as well. We would meet Chandram Chowan, a 65-year-old man whom the Banjaras call Guruji, or teacher. The settlement, a successful experiment financially supported by the government, houses some 3,000 Banjaras. The whitewashed arch at the entrance had its name painted on it: The Nehru Nagar Banjara Centre. Guruji sat in his office surrounded by his collaborators. Our arrival and the idea of a book on the Gypsies pleased him tremendously. "You can see and photograph everything – we have worked very hard to achieve this," he said. As we walked past the first row of small whitewashed houses, with little drainage conduits in front of them, the Gypsies came out to bow to their benefactor. The village, we learned from Guruji, has schools in which the children are taught English and Maraka, the language spoken locally. All the teachers are Banjaras, except for the pretty Sushila Abuta, an untouchable, one of the rare members of this lowest caste who has managed to become educated and get a teaching post. The children are given a free meal at school. Of the 5,000 children who have attended this school so far, some 200 have managed to gain university degrees in various parts of India. Some have become doctors and occasionally come to the village to help with health and hygiene education. The village has an agricultural commune organized on land bought with government aid. At the frequent village meetings, they discuss everything, even family planning. This was welcomed by the Banjara women who, as a result, have only three to four children each, unlike their tribeswomen elsewhere who, on average, give birth to about ten. Each member of this community has a job or duty. Walking through the village, we noticed that the children did not run after us asking for money, that there were fewer dogs...

When we left the village, Rajko commented on what we had seen, from the point of view of a sociologist: "Naturally, when you get a lot of homeless people together, feed them and organize them, it can function, on this low level. They are happy to work and do as they're told. If you try to do the same in a slightly more developed community, the results are disastrous."

We continued our journey along a secondary road running through an agricultural area towards the Deccan plain. We told Ranjit that, after seeing an organized settlement, we now wished to visit the Banjaras' traditional villages. "Even if you wanted to see another place like this one, it would be impossible – it's unique. Their other villages belong to another age; nothing has changed in their lives for countless generations. Some are still nomads, while others live on the outskirts of towns, mostly in the Deccan plain. They work as seasonal laborers for a miserable wage or practice one of the dozen or so crafts they inherited with their caste."

The sun blazed down and our driver had to stop even more often to cool the engine, while we waited impatiently. During one such halt, we saw a group of Banjara women working in the fields, threshing sugar cane. Zamur hid behind a bush and took shots through a telescopic lens of the women, bent double, treading the cane and spreading it out with their hands amid clouds of dust. When he signaled that he had finished, we set off over the field toward the women. Some fifty yards away from them we were met by the only man in sight, their overseer from the sugar refinery. There were two groups, each of about a hundred women, working separately. We asked the overseer why

44   Dogs are part of the Gypsy "milieu" throughout India. Hundreds of hounds are the joint property, so to speak, of each Gypsy camp. "Where there are Gypsies," says a Gypsy proverb, "there must be fires and hounds." Dogs are a part of their lives, and share whatever there is to eat. They run around free and rarely fight among themselves, but jointly attack any stranger who dares to approach the settlement, as we discovered to our cost.

this was so. ''The Gypsies refuse to work with the untouchables, who are below them in caste,'' he answered. ''Everyone knows his place here in India. It has always been this way; it's nothing new.'' Though we were now very near them, the women labored on, coming closer, bent over, not raising their heads. We asked the overseer to stop them, and he did so. When they straightened up, Zamur took a few fast shots. It was not until the dust had somewhat settled that we noticed they were carrying their babies with them, as well as wearing all their jewelry, which, according to Ranjit, can weigh up to 12 pounds. The overseer told us they brought their own food and water, and worked a fifteen-hour day for five rupees (c. 40 US cents).

Traveling on along the narrow, dusty road full of potholes, we came to the village of Balogy Nagar Tanda, some 50 miles from Sholapur. By now we had left the agricultural area and entered the arid Deccan plain. It is said that in the 14th century the Great Moghul collected Gypsies from the north and made them bearers of weapons and supplies for his armies. Thus they came to this plain and stayed here. We waited at a respectful distance for Ranjit to return from the village. It transpired that this day there was to be a celebration in honor of Kali Durga (the Black Virgin) who, according to legend, was Shiva's wife. This goddess, represented wearing a necklace of human skulls, is the patron of children. While Ranjit conferred with the Gypsies, we devised a strategy that would allow Zamur to photograph everything undisturbed and unseen with this telescopic lens. With Rajko and Ranjit holding the attention of the Gypsies, Zamur and I slipped away unnoticed in the commotion to enter the village from the opposite side. We climbed a convenient tree from where, well hidden, we enjoyed an excellent view of the whole event. The Gypsies, divided into two groups, circled the village in a sort of procession, one group leading an ox, the offering to the goddess. After much singing and dancing by the women, the now unified procession moved on again towards the shrine of Kali Durga, where there was more singing and dancing: according to Ranjit, they were calling on the Gypsy spirits to protect them from evil and sickness. Although officially Hindus, these Banjaras have retained much of their own pagan faith.

We spent two more days on the Deccan plateau, which is dotted with Banjara villages, and slept in our bags near the car – a much better solution than repeating the discomforts of Sholapur. Here we had a feeling that the air and ground were clean, unlike down in the lowlands. Our encounters with the Gypsies of the Deccan were among the most fascinating experiences of our trip. They live in tiny huts like conical bee-hives, with walls of daub and wattle. Each of these huts can be built in a single day, and obviously serves simply as a place to sleep: the Gypsies' lives are lived outdoors, so they have no need for anything more spacious. In front of each hut was a neat pile of cow dung, fuel for the fire around which they sit and cook. We sat with them until far into the night, listening to Ranjit's conversation with them. The women heaped up and lit the dry dung – it burned slowly and smoked a lot. Then they baked *roti*, a kind of flat round bread made from dough shaped by beating with the palms. Like most other Indians, they hardly ever eat meat, and *roti*, in addition to rice and vegetables, which are plentiful, is the mainstay of their diet.

As we sat with them beneath the star-studded sky, the Gpysy women started singing. Then they rose, took two or three steps around the fire and broke into a dance, their skirts slowly swinging, their arms raised. Banjara dancing has no instrumental accompaniment, only the rhythmic jingling of the little bells on the women's anklets. For hours the singing echoed over the Deccan plain. This, Rajko explained, was supposed to strengthen the collective spirit. ''What we are watching now, I have seen in settlements near

Belgrade hundreds of times. Gypsies do it all over the world. They brought the tradition with them from India and it's connected to the fire ritual, to Duwali, Holi and Teej."

Ranjit was just as interested to hear about Gypsies in other parts of the world as we were to learn about those in India, and we discovered many similarities in their way of life. We learned that during Holi an effigy of Lord Khama is burned while the Gypsies sing and dance until sunrise.

In one hut we were taken to, we came upon two women with a small child lying in a basket. The baby, clearly sick, cried continuously, while the older woman waved her arms over it, chanting. The mother told Ranjit that her child had a fever and, fearing it would die, she had summoned the sorceress. The high infant mortality made women dependent on the sorceresses, we were told by Ranjit. We fetched some aspirin and antibiotics from our first-aid bag and asked Ranjit to tell the mother that her child might get better from what we had to offer. She looked interested, but the sorceress watched us suspiciously, obviously displeased at having competition. To avoid friction, we urged her to finish her "cure", but asked that our medicine should be given a chance as well. Some of the tablets had to be taken every six hours. Remembering that the Banjaras had no clocks and told the time by the sun, we explained that a capsule should be mixed with milk and given to the child at sunrise, when the sun was high, at sundown and after the fire was put out. On leaving we wondered whether the child would recover, but all the same we continued our journey feeling we had done a good deed.

Next we headed for Shivaggy Nagar Tanda, a village of some thirty mud huts with thatched roofs and earthen floors covered with rush mats. Ranjit had chosen it because he knew the chief. Here we were lucky again: on this day the village celebrated Kali Durga by sacrificing a black goat. The priest dissolved cow dung in water and then painted the area around the little shrine with this mixture. All this time the women stood round watching, and when he had finished, started singing, first quietly, then louder and more rythmically. "They are calling on their forefathers," Ranjit explained, "mentioning their names and good deeds and asking for protection. For the Gypsies the ancestors are always present, and their help and advice are often sought on matters concerning their present life. The future they try to read from palms and other means of fortune-telling." Two women, a little apart from the rest, sang by themselves, as though unconnected with the others. The priest worked on, drawing signs with whitewash on the dung-soaked area: first a cross, then two parallel lines on each side, then a few other symbols, the swastika among them.

The goat was brought forward. The priest took a bowl of water and a green twig and sprinkled the animal's head. It did not react. He repeated the "baptism", and this time the goat shook its head, making the women sing louder and faster. Ranjit told us that by shaking its head the goat had given assent for its sacrifice to Kali Durga, without which it could not be slaughtered — it sometimes happened that an animal was stubborn and the sprinkling went on for hours! Then the goat was led to the symbols and slaughtered. When the blood poured out on to the signs, one of the two women who had sung alone fell to the ground in a trance resembling an epileptic fit. The other lay over her and invoked the spirits of the ancestors.

When the goat was dead, the priest first cut off the head and placed it in the middle of the cross, for all to see, then chopped off the legs and put each on one of the lines. Next the goat's heart was laid on the swastika, an old Gypsy symbol. Accompanied by singing and chanting, the whole animal was gradually cut up, every piece of meat being dedicated to an ancestor, in order to humor and honor him. In the end they were all placed in a cauldron to boil.

Perhaps fortunately, we could not wait for the end of the celebration, when the meat was to be eaten – we had to continue our trip. Ranjit told us that on such occasions everybody got drunk on palm wine and the festivities frequently ended with a fight or even murder. Today the latter case is dealt with by the police, but everything else is judged according to Gypsy law and tradition by a five-man council: the elder, the Naik, and four other senior members of the tribe. Women have no part in these proceedings. He gave us examples of the way in which the council works: in the case of theft from another Gypsy, the guilty person pays a fine; in the case of rape, he is thrown out of the village; if a wife is unfaithful, she also has to leave the village and her family must return the money received for her; if a husband is unfaithful, he pays a fine. Polygamy is still practiced, though gradually disappearing. Family relationship is recognized only on the male line: cousins on the mother's side may marry, but not on the father's. When a woman is widowed, her husband's brother takes her to wife even if he is already married. All these are Banjara customs.

After several days of traveling, with many stops to cool the engine or replace a flat tire, we came to Hyderabad. On a hill above the town rises a luxury hotel – the Banjara. It acquired its name from the fact that the hill had previously been inhabited by Gypsies, who were moved to the foot. No longer filthy and unshaven, we spent a wonderful evening on the terrace of the hotel. As we sipped our cold beer next to wealthy foreign tourists, we had a strange feeling of having stepped out of the past into the present.

Next morning, refreshed and relaxed, we set off towards Kurnool to visit a few more villages before flying north to New Delhi and seeking out the Gypsies of the Punjab and Rajasthan. These villages were in Andhra Pradesh state, and we were interested to discover whether there were any differences in the way Gypsies lived there. Soon after leaving Hyderabad we came across a Banjara village of about 600 huts and 3,000 inhabitants named Dever Kina. A man from here, we were told, had been elected to the Hyderabad city council. In the last few years, the Banjaras from the city outskirts had become politically active. They supported Indira Gandhi's party because she had shown the most understanding for their problems. Many were employed in Hyderabad and in a much better position than their brothers in the Bombay power-station settlement. We were informed, with pride, that some of the villagers had obtained university degrees. It was clear that these ghetto people were now fighting for the improvement of their lot.

We watched Banjara women making long skirts, stitching tiny round mirrors onto them. Some were for their own use, some for sale in the town, where tourists are interested in buying Gypsy skirts. These can have as many as 2,000 mirrors on them, and weigh up to 12 pounds. Sewing on that many mirrors takes 60 days, working eight hours a day. When asked why they needed such richly ornamented skirts, the Gypsy women said they wanted their daughters to be respected in the village. The skirts did not serve to enhance the girls' beauty, only the respect they received. ''A woman has no use for beauty,'' one Gypsy seamstress told us. ''Only the man who buys her has some good of that.'' Did she think a woman should be allowed to choose her own husband? ''The men will never allow that. They are stronger than women and if we refused the man chosen for us, we would be beaten into submission.'' We asked whether wives were at least consulted about the children and how many they wanted. ''That depends on the man.''

Some 60 miles from Hyderabad we visited three Gypsy settlements: Dintapalli Tanda, Kurmeth Tanda and Chernoraum Tanda. In the first village we discussed the Banjaras' caste position. We asked them whether they were still discriminated against, persecuted and considered members of the crimi-

84

nal tribe. They replied that although the caste system did not favor them, at least they were not untouchables. There was someone below them, and that was good. Their elders went to Kurnool and other towns in the vicinity to arrange for work as seasonal laborers, building roads and houses and carrying baskets of earth, sand and stones on their heads. The men work together with their wives, but being stronger, receive double the pay. Despite the burning heat, ''etiquette'' demands that the woman wear all her clothes, while the man can strip to cool off. In the evening we sat by the fire, listening to the lament of the Banjara women and watching their ritual rain dance. They told us about the tattooing which is obligatory among the Banjaras. The women are marked on the nose, forehead, arms and legs, the tattoos differing from one tribal group to another.

We returned to Hyderabad, from where we flew to New Delhi. Ranjit flew with us, but then had to say goodbye: he could not accompany us any further as his health was too precarious for the blistering heat of the Rajasthan desert.

Rajko had arranged for J. S. Pathania, who lived in Jammu, Kashmir, to accompany us further on our trip. As agreed, Pathania waited for us at a hotel. He had only just arrived and was exhausted, unshaven and in a highly agitated state. ''There's a real war going on between the Sikhs and the army in Punjab,'' he said. The previous night he had been obliged to dodge patrols as martial law had been declared and a curfew imposed. Caught by some soldiers near the railway station, he had had great trouble persuading them to let him travel to New Delhi. There had been fifty dead that day in Jammu. Pathania had spent 20 hours in a train so as not to let us down.

Like Ranjit, he too was striving to improve the position of the Gypsies, in Punjab, Jammu and Kashmir, where they are mostly nomads or semi-nomadic, herding goats and buffaloes. Some of the Gypsy families, he told us, have as many as 1,000 goats. The head of such a wealthy family usually becomes one of the tribal elders. The women's attire differs from that of the Banjaras. They usually wear a necklace of silver or some other metal, from which hang two picks – one for the ears, the other for the teeth. This constitutes their sole possession: everything else belongs to the men, who each have several wives, and look rather Afghan in appearance, thin and angular. Before the division in 1947 they used to move to Afghanistan and Pakistan with their herds, but that has had to stop. All the Gypsy tribes who live in the northern states originated in Rajasthan, from the areas of Jodhpur and Jaipur. They marry early, as do other Gypsies, usually paying 2,000 rupees or 50 goats for a wife, though sometimes a woman can cost as much as 70,000 rupees (6,000 US dollars), a real fortune by their standards. Pathania recounted a case in his region of a young man who fell in love with a married woman in a neighboring village. He let the husband know that he wished to buy her from him, but the latter, also valuing his wife's beauty, set the price at 70,000 rupees. The young man's family and the whole village pooled their money and raised the sum. Bound by his word, the husband had to hand over his wife. The tale of this Gypsy Helen of Troy thus ended without warring, although according to Pathania, it is not rare for these wild people to fight over a woman.

The owner of 1,000 goats is called *Pir* – "leader" in Persian. He also cures the sick, whereas among the Banjaras that is the prerogative of sorcerers. The healing generally takes the form of the elder blowing on some water and giving it to the sick person to drink – supposedly this treatment is often effective. At the same time the elder prays to Allah (the Gypsies in this part of India are Moslem): if the sick man has been righteous and God wills it, he will

B. A. Bolswert
after D. Vinckboons:
Engraving.
D. Ternois, ''L'art de J. Callot'',
(Paris, 1962)

be cured – if not, he will die. The Pir is only Allah's representative and can not be held responsible for the results.

Arguments between Gypsies are also settled by the Pir. Pathania recalled witnessing a fight between two groups of Gypsies in which one man was killed. The village leader (Mukadam) decided that the murderer was to serve the wife of the victim until her children were of age, and tend her goats. He was forbidden to marry her or sleep with her, this being against Gypsy law. "To kill in return," the Gypsy leader said, " will not solve the problem of feeding the dead man's children."

There are two kinds of Gypsy nomads in northwest India, Pathania told us: those who continually travel, and those who move around only in summer and return in winter to the same sites. The Moslem Gypsies, the Goyars and Bokerwals, numbering up to a million, bury their dead, whilst the Hindu cremate them, unless the deceased are children, old people or holy men, who are interred. In Jammu there are a few educated Gypsies. Some serve in the Indian army, but if they become officers, they repudiate any connection with Gypsies, and usually call themselves Khans – Afghan warriors who, although extremely poor, are esteemed for their courage and excellence as soldiers.

In this part of the world the Gypsies are terrified of ghosts and evil spirits. Since these are believed to be particularly active on nights of the full moon, the Gypsies avoid going anywhere at such times. Pathania recounted how he himself almost died because of ghosts. He was working at the time on some British oil drills. Around his tent the sand was so fresh and smooth that even a tiny lizard left a trail, yet the tent was visited by a ghost who left none. Pathania moved his tent elsewhere, but his friend stayed. The following day he fell ill, and told Pathania that he had seen a ghost. Pathania tried to convince him he had only been dreaming, but the man died a few days later. "He was 35," Pathania recalled, "strong and healthy. A priest came with holy water, but nothing helped."

Then he told us of another occasion when he almost lost his life in the desert. While working on an oil drill, he glanced up and had a premonition that the two-ton weight used to press the drill would fall. It was the time of full moon. He told the British overseer of this feeling but the man told him to keep working – he would take care of the evil spirits. Pathania, however, lost his nerve and left the drill. When the Englishman called him back, he had to return to his post, but as he approached, the weight fell with a tremendous crash. Pathania was unharmed, but the overseer was crushed to death. "We Gypsies have the sixth sense and this often saves our lives. The more faith one has, the stronger one's sixth sense."

He also described how Gypsies use large lizards, goannas, for theft: they tie a rope to the reptile's tail and throw it over a wall. The creature clings to the wall with its claws, and the Gypsies climb the rope attached to its tail. The Boria Gypsies consider the goanna a delicacy and serve it to visitors. It is a great insult to refuse such a special dish, and guests may come to harm if they do so.

Pathania was full of fascinating stories of the Gypsies' life in northern India. We were therefore very disappointed when he announced that he wanted to return to Jammu, as our Punjab trip was clearly out of the question, but would gladly accompany us some other year. "It is dangerous even for me to go there, let alone for you, foreigners. Nobody would be responsible if something happened to you, and there are criminals on the loose who would kill you for a single dollar. Apart from this, there are barricades on the roads. It is better for you to go to Rajasthan, which is more important for the book."

We said goodbye to Pathania and were left to our own resources. Nada Ahuja saved the day yet again. A 19-year-old relative of her husband's,

Sundeep Jethany, agreed to act as our guide. We asked him to get us a van and a good English-speaking driver, but this was no easier in New Delhi than in Bombay, he told us, and we ageed to the 1939 model Ford, as long as it was new and didn't overheat so often. The agency he spoke to sent us a car and driver to try out for a day, sight-seeing around the city, before we hired them for the trip. The driver's English was quite good, and the car almost new. More important, Nada's relative was an intelligent and efficient young man who knew Rajasthan well and could tell us a great deal about the desert Gypsies. We decided, with his agreement, to try getting to Punjab despite the warnings: we could always turn off towards Rajasthan if the going got rough. We arranged to leave very early the following morning.

Impatient and excited before the trip, we were at the reception desk at 3 a.m. Car and driver also turned up, but not those from the day before: this driver spoke no English, and the vehicle was not as new. Sundeep argued angrily, but in vain. Resigned, we set off northwards, through the state of Haryana. About midday we were overtaken by military trucks and a few police cars, but we pressed on along the dusty road, meeting Gypsies in carts drawn by oxen or camels going to fairs to sell their copper and iron wares. We stopped occasionally to take a few photographs and chat to them.

Approaching the Punjab border, we had to drive slowly behind light armored vehicles. We passed two military patrols who let us by without asking questions, probably thinking we were making for a nearby town. When we stopped for the night, we consulted the hotel manager. He considered it was too risky to continue as there were barricades near the next village, manned by several hundred people, who prevented any traffic from passing. We learned, however, that they went home at night and returned to their positions at about 10 a.m. Accustomed to early rising to get the best light, we decided to set out before dawn. On two or three occasions we stopped to photograph Gypsies who had pitched their tents near the road. "They pass all the frontiers and troubles of the world with ease, and no barricades can stop them," Rajko commented. These belonged to the Sansi, a group of smugglers. Any emergency or crisis suited them as it was bound to cause a shortage of something they could procure across the border, smuggle in and sell at great profit. On the Pakistan frontier members of this tribe, either ignorant or heedless of the dangers, smuggle drugs for the big dealers.

Chatting to the Gypsies on this sunny morning, we suddenly realized that it was already 9 a.m. and left hurriedly, driving the next 20 miles at top speed. Approaching a large village, we saw a mass of people some 100 yards ahead. Catching sight of our car, the defenders of the barricade started angrily shouting, waving their arms and wielding sticks. When some began running towards us with threatening gestures, we all yelled at the driver to stop, but he continued driving as though spellbound. Shouting frantically, we finally got him to turn into a narrow side street, since a truck behind us made it impossible to reverse. There we were soon surrounded by an irate throng, seemingly intent on lynching us. Our driver appeared inclined to get out and talk matters over, but we yelled at him to keep going. Having pushed through this crowd, we next found a truck blocking our way a 100 yards further on, near a crossroads. In a moment another mob had swamped us and started banging on the roof of our car with sticks, and trying to open the doors. By reversing we eventually managed to get on to a path leading through some fields.

As luck would have it, we soon came upon the main road which would take us to Rajasthan. For a while all went well, and we had already recovered somewhat from our ordeal when 200 yards ahead loomed another barricade. This time the driver needed no prompting! But just as he was reversing, there

45 *Afghanistan, the first country on the Gypsies' route westward from their homeland, was too poor and barren for many to stay. Only some 20,000 can be found here today, the majority nomads. Their most common occupation is making sieves and wooden objects, such as the musical instruments in the picture.*

46 Close to the border with Iran a group of nomadic Gypsies has camped for the night. Beside the most numerous tribe, the Ghorbati, there are several others in Afghanistan: Jalili, Pikraj, Shadibaz and Vangauala, all of them collectively called Jat. (pp 90-1)

*47, 48 The Gypsies of Afghanistan are
forbidden to settle in or near towns and
generally suffer discrimination. Their worldly
goods loaded on camels, they move around
doing odd jobs for the Afghan peasants.
The harsh climate and poor nutrition result in
short life expectancy among the nomads, and
high infant mortality.*

49 The Gypsy population of Iran today numbers about 100,000. According to the Arab historian Hamza of Isfahan, writing in c. 950, the first group arrived in Persia in AD 420. Said to have come from India, they were called Lur by the Persians.

50, 51 Most Iranian Gypsies are nomadic, moving around in groups and often mixing with Iranian nomads such as the Beseri, for whom they provide blacksmith services. They also make sieves, weave rugs and perform as musicians and dancers. They have adopted the Shi-ite Moslem religion while preserving some of their pagan beliefs and rituals.

52 The settled Gypsies in Iran are known as Abdali, while the nomads belong to the Kouli, Ghorbati and Fiuj tribes. The authorities are intolerant towards the Gypsies, and many leave Iran for neighboring countries. (pp. 96–97)

53

55

*53, 54   Apart from the language of the host
country, Iranian Gypsies also use a language
formed by a mixture of dialects, mostly
spoken by tribes which came from
Baluchistan and Afghanistan or which
formerly lived in Armenia. This tongue bears
little resemblance to the Romany of the
European Gypsies.*

*55   Leather bellows are worked by the
women to keep up a red-hot heat for the
blacksmith to forge implements.*

56 Sizable groups of Gypsies live on the outskirts of Teheran and Shiraz. Many of them make a living as musicians, singers and dancers, like their ancestors who came to perform at the court of the Persian ruler 15 centuries ago. At feasts and festivals, the colorfully dressed Gypsy dancers are much in demand.

57 In Izmir (Smyrna) we met this little Gypsy, temporarily separated by the traffic from his group, which had come from the interior to sell their copper and iron wares at a fair. The Gypsy population of Turkey, now some half a million, was first counted in a late-15th century Ottoman census, when it numbered 60,000.

58, 59   In Istanbul several thousand
Gypsies earn their living by shining shoes,
drawing the attention of prospective
customers by banging their brushes against
the shoe-box. As the competition is fierce,
many use cunning tricks to attract trade. As
Zamur was walking along the street, a little
Gypsy pointed out that his shoes were dirty,
and Zamur was puzzled to see that there was
indeed fresh mud on them although the
streets were dry. Never mind, the little
Gypsy just happened to have a shoeshine
friend . . . In the background: the church of
Haghia Sophia.

60, 62 Gypsies in Turkey often work as seasonal laborers in the cotton fields. These photographs have tragic associations, for while we were taking them, our Gypsy guide, Elmaz, was knocked down and fatally injured by a truck.

61 Gypsy nomads near Kuçukkuyu, close to Izmir. Basket-weaving is a traditional Gypsy craft, still practiced in all the countries where they live. Its advantage is the abundance of raw material available on the river banks by which they camp. Their laundry, shopping and bread baskets are sold door to door or at open-air markets in towns. This group told us they had twice tried to cross over into Greece, believing their wares would sell better there, but on both occasions they had been caught and turned back by the Turkish authorities.

63, 64 In the Kervan Serai night club in the European part of Istanbul, we sat among the tourists and Turkish guests and watched belly-dancing performed by pretty Gypsy girls. Three of them took it in turn to dance, then came among the audience, climbed on to the tables laden with food and drink and continued gyrating, to the accompaniment of tambourines and a kind of clarinet. Some of the guests, mostly Turks, roared approval, waved their arms and stuffed wads of money into the dancers' brassieres and belts. Only a few Gypsy dancers have the good fortune to perform in tourist traps and good cabarets: the majority never progress beyond the little bars scattered throughout Turkey.

65   Sulukule is a Gypsy ghetto beside the northern walls of Istanbul. With its reputation for wild night life, it is frequented mostly by sailors. We were warned that no self-respecting and sensible Turk would go there after dark. Ahmed, our Turkish guide, had to be cajoled into taking us through the dim-lit narrow alleys to a little house from which floated the muffled strains of oriental music. We sat down in a corner of the bar as the dancers were being introduced, the woman proprietor intimating that for an additional charge customers could get more than just dancing.

66 The owner served the guests with orange segments, nuts and a murky-looking liquid. Ahmed was the only one to drink it, while the rest of us, ever cautious, merely pretended to sip. A few minutes later Ahmed collapsed under the table and the lights went out. We jumped up and stood with our backs against the wall. When the Gypsies realized that only one of us had passed out and that their "doctored" drinks had not worked very well that night, the lights came back on. We beat a hasty retreat, half-carrying and half-dragging Ahmed out of the ghetto the same way we had come.

67, 69 Greece was the first stopping-place for Gypsies when they reached Europe in the 11th century, or perhaps earlier. They traveled, in smaller and larger groups, along the famous Roman Via Egnatia, nowadays overgrown from disuse, for asphalt roads have replaced it.

*68   This group of nomadic Gypsies were
camped near the ruins of the ancient
Macedonian town of Philippi. After
a successful day selling smuggled goods at
the local market, they celebrated by dancing
and singing. George Tramaris demonstrated
his acrobatic skill to Bato Tomašević. With
a number of fellow Gypsies, he earns his
living as a street entertainer. When the police
arrive, they move elsewhere. "We are
Christians, Orthodox," George told us. "We
behave and dress just like the Greeks, except
that we don't go to church."*

70, 71   *George Tramaris invited us to share his supper: hedgehog Gypsy style. We watched his friend Spiros blow into the animal's rectum through a straw until it died. This way, he explained, the flesh was much tastier than when the hedgehog was slaughtered. "When you blow," Spiros said, "the skin separates from the meat and can be easily removed." That evening there was a Gypsy gathering, and a dozen or so hedgehogs and several snakes were prepared and served, along with beer and whisky.*

72 The Moslem Gypsy settlement in Xanthi, near the Turkish border, has been a kind of transit station for Turkish Gypsies for many years. The inhabitants have strong ties with Turkey and practice their faith, worshipping at the mosque, unlike their Orthodox brethren, who rarely go to church. As usual, our appearance in the place drew swarms of excited children.

73 In the Gypsy settlement in Drama we were invited to Akis's house, a hut built and whitewashed by himself and his wife. The settlement has no running water or electricity. Akis provides for his wife and three children by collecting scrap-iron and paper. In summer, when there are more tourists, he also sells souvenirs in the street. We were offered Greek coffee, prepared on a little gas cooker outside the hut.

74 In the Dendrapotamos ghetto on the outskirts of Salonika, we talked to Yiannis, the Gypsy elder. He told us that 90% of the Gypsies living there earned their living as street vendors, a few were market traders, and the rest worked in factories or collected garbage and scrap-iron. The settlement has existed since the middle of the last century,

when these Gypsies' forefathers settled here after being banished from the Middle East. Yiannis is one of the Gypsies fighting for the right to use their own language, have their own schools, radio and newspapers. Most of the houses in the settlement are tidy and painted blue, like Yiannis's in the picture.

75   In Komotini, a small town near Kavala, we came upon a settlement of Moslem Gypsies. Our arrival, without a guide to announce and introduce us, was definitely not welcomed by the men. Luckily, they did not grasp at first that we wanted to take photographs of their womenfolk, so we managed to snap Sabia, who was washing laundry with a group of girls, before we made a hasty departure.

was a commotion on the barricade: people started clambering over it and running in all directions. When the mass had thinned out, we could see police vans from which policemen armed with batons were leaping out and chasing the rebels. In an instant there was nobody left at the barricade except the police, busy removing the boulders and branches from the road. We drove past the surprised policemen and headed towards Rajasthan. Pathania had been right, after all.

We finally got to the Rajasthan desert, an eternity of sand stretching as far as the eye could see in all directions, burned by a merciless sun. Rajko was excited – we had come at last to the home of all Gypsies, the source from which they had streamed into the world in search of a better life. We decided to try and cross into Pakistan as tourists: we had applied to the Embassy in Belgrade for visas, but were refused on the grounds that ''there are no Gypsies or tribes related to them on the territory of Pakistan.'' Rajko insisted that there were: he even knew some personally and had their addresses.

We passed through Bikaner, where we left our car and driver and set off in a hired Jeep toward Anupparh. Just a few miles out of Bikaner we were caught up in long lines of military vehicles and the closer we got to the border the more often we saw army encampments. We agreed to forget about entering Pakistan for the moment, and try crossing again at Jaisalmer. Having turned back, we came upon a group of some 200 Lohar Gypsies, their donkeys laden with tents and copperware, heading towards the border. This, we learned, was their fourth day of traveling across the blistering sands. They were leading several hounds on long leashes: the only dogs in India that had owners, it seemed to us. Sundeep told us they were sight hounds, used for hunting gazelles and hares. When the Gypsies spot some game ahead, they release the dogs and soon have roast meat for supper. However, in this desert live the Bistnoi people, strict vegetarians who, in their defence of nature, will not allow even a branch to be cut in their presence. If the Bistnoi caught the Gypsies hunting, they would kill both them and their dogs: according to their beliefs, nature must not be destroyed, but men who do so deserve to be killed. For this reason the Gypsies had tied up their dogs.

We set off towards Jaisalmer across the starkly beautiful desert and soon encountered a handful of Banjara Gypsies expertly driving almost a thousand camels: centuries of this work has taught them to run ahead and cut off any animals trying to stray. Sundeep told us that they were camel-traders who sold the animals for their owners. They go from village to village until they have sold them all, which can take up to a year. Trading in animals, especially horses, is a traditional Gypsy occupation in Europe, too, as Rajko pointed out.

We saw many temporary Gypsy settlements along the way. The tiny mud huts, surrounded by a fence of thorny branches, resembled swallows' nests scattered on the sands. As Sundeep did not speak their dialect, we crept up to them and took as many fast shots as possible. The women, alone in the villages during the day, covered their faces from strangers. We watched them weaving cloth on primitive looms of a type in use for thousands of years, and dyeing cotton brilliant red, yellow and blue colors.

Unlike southern India, where there are only Banjara Gypsies, in the north there are members of all tribes. The Banjaras are to be found in Rajasthan as well, herding or trading cattle, working as seasonal laborers or acrobats; the Gaduliya Lohar are smiths, the Jogi musicians, the Sansi and Khanjar traders and smugglers.

That evening we stayed in a hotel in Jaisalmer, and sat up listening to Jogi musicians: two or three drums and simple flutes or pipes, a singer and a tall, very dark-skinned dancer. It was she who collected money from the audience, stuffing it down the front of her blouse. Having no change, I gave her a 50-rupee note (4 US dollars). Soon after, we went to our room, knowing we had an early start. A few minutes later, there was a knock at our door and on opening it, we found the Gypsy dancer, who obviously thought we were expecting more than music for that amount of money. We managed to bundle her out of the room, but not before parting with a bottle of after-shave in response to her request for "perfume"... Thus we encountered another of the old professions related to singing and dancing.

Before dawn we were standing on a hill in front of the 13th-century fortress of Jaisalmer, the mecca of tourists. A few minutes before sunrise a group of Jogi Gypsy musicians arrived to entertain sightseers, as their ancestors had entertained the rulers of the fortress in bygone times. Their musical instruments were of ancient, primitive type, made of half a coconut, bamboo, and donkey hair. Sitting on the hill, listening to their strange, haunting music, we decided we had had enough adventures for the time being and would not attempt to cross into Pakistan after all. We would go to Jodhpur and return, via Ajmer and Jaipur, to New Delhi, and then to Europe.

Our trip, we decided, had been successful. Among other aspects, it had been interesting to discover the various professions of Gypsies in India – professions they had taken with them on their endless travels and still practice today, ten centuries later.

Sundeep asked whether we wanted to visit an area where Gypsies trained monkeys and bears, but dazed by our impressions, our nervous energy exhausted, we reluctantly declined. Rajko answered jokingly: "That we can see on the outskirts of Belgrade!"

Turkey

Estimated number: 500,000
Main centers: Istanbul, Ankara, Izmir
Language: Romany
Religion: Moslem
Tribal group: Arlije

Turkey, the bridge between two continents, crossed by the Gypsies on their travels to Europe, left a strong imprint on a large section of them – on their music, religion, way of life... Just before we were to leave, however, an unexpected problem arose: Rajko Djurić could not accompany us, feeling unable to refuse an invitation from the University of Heidelberg to spend three months there, studying the situation and problems of Gypsies in West Germany. As there are several tens of thousands of Gypsies from all over Europe and Turkey among the "guest workers" in Germany, the Bonn government had decided to try and help them adapt to their new environment and socialize them. It was not possible to wait until Rajko's return, so furnished with the address of a certain Osman in Izmir who, according to our Viennese connection, spoke excellent English, Zamur and I decided to go it alone.

However, we had a problem – should we fail to find Osman, how were we, two male Gadjas, who spoke neither Turkish nor Romany, to approach the Gypsies and photograph them and their womenfolk without being attacked or knifed by jealous husbands?

"If we had a woman with us, it would be much easier," Zamur said. "She could approach them first, put them in a better mood. That always works in Moslem countries. That way the Gypsies won't immediately think we have some designs on their women." Hearing this, my daughter, Una, seized at the chance of going to Turkey and offered her services as secretary and sandwich-maker. We also invited along the 25-year-old son of some English friends, Richard Holland, who was staying in Belgrade for a few days on a round-the-world trip: the more the merrier, and also the safer.

We all set off in a hired Volkswagen van. On the way, Zamur and

I entertained the two young people with anecdotes from our earlier travels, and discussed all we could photograph in Turkey. We planned to visit Istanbul and take photographs of Gypsy women doing the belly-dance, which we could then contrast with photos of the Spanish Flamenco dancers and the Gypsies who dance on the streets and squares of India. In Istanbul we would also photograph the shoeshine boys and the porters in the harbor, saddled with loads as heavy as their Gypsy backs could take. In Izmir, where there are about 10,000 Gypsies, we would have to photograph the cockfights which the Gypsies organize and on which they are prepared to stake all their earthly possessions. We were most excited, though, at the prospect of visiting the underdeveloped areas of Turkey where Gypsies work for fifteen hours a day as cotton-pickers on the Anatolian plain, and the settlements in the hills inhabited by backward and wild Gypsies who keep bears, monkeys and other animals with which they travel around to fairs. But only the men, since their women still wear the veil, even though the Turks themselves, from whom they adopted the custom, long ago abolished it.

Chatting cheerfully, we passed through Bulgaria (the shortest possible route from Belgrade) without stopping. Approaching the border, we left the subject of Gypsies for a while and moved to discussing everything we knew about Turkey. Richard mentioned "Midnight Express", a film we had all seen, Una talked of the drug route, Zamur of the prisons into which people were thrown for traffic misdemeanors or causing accidents. As he was driving, we all advised him to be specially careful, just in case. We had heard tales of some unfortunates who had languished forgotten in Turkish prisons for years, until nobody could even remember why they were supposed to be there. Seeing the Turkish soldiers at the approach to the border, with their helmets, shaven heads, long coats and boots, I could not help remembering that for centuries my Montenegrin forefathers had fought ceaselessly against the Ottoman armies. We filled in all the forms, showed the documents for the van, and entered Turkey with very little trouble.

In Istanbul, our first stop, we visited Sulukule, a Gypsy ghetto, where we had one of our more hair-raising experiences (see picture captions). In contrast, we joined tourists in an up-market night club where the more fortunate Gypsy belly-dancers find employment.

Next we set off for Izmir, heading south-west towards Gelibolu (Gallipoli) and across the Dardanelles.

Entering Izmir, the third largest city and the second largest port after Istanbul, we tried not to get nervous while weaving our way through the exceptionally lively and unpredictable traffic. Now we faced the daunting task of locating, on one of the hills on which Izmir is built, the home of our Gypsy connection, Osman. We had obtained his address from his brother-in-law, Moses, who lives in Vienna. Osman, he said, could take us to Gypsy settlements, show us how they live and arrange for photographing with the wild Gypsies in the hills. Crawling through the crowded, narrow and very steep streets, we had to stop every few minutes to ask the way, turn around, let other vehicles pass. When we eventually got stuck in front of a flight of steps, we decided to continue the search on foot. Leaving Una and Richard to look after our things, Zamur and I wandered through the narrow alleys, up and down steps, until at last we came upon Osman's little house, set inside a courtyard and almost invisible from the street. It consisted of one room only, small but tidy, reached by descending several steps. At the door we took off our shoes, as is the custom in Turkey. Osman and his wife were having a rest after lunch, but seeing strangers enter, rose immediately. On hearing us mention Moses, their faces broke into smiles of welcome.

I at once set about explaining why we had come, how Moses had given us the address, and the trouble we'd had finding it. "Moses," Osman said, and I repeated it, only then realizing, with dismay, that this was the sole word he had understood. Incredulous, we tried to get Osman to speak English, but to no avail: he could count to ten, say "yes" and "no", and that was about all — as a street-vendor of little plastic souvenirs, he had never needed to learn more. Clearly he would be no use as an interpreter. Sitting opposite each other, we all repeated "Moses good, Fatima good," but that was the limit of our communication. It was not the first time that someone recommended by Gypsies as speaking a language "perfectly" had turned out to know only a few words, but before we had had Rajko with us and his command of Romany had solved the problem. Just as we were thinking of leaving, a smiling young Gypsy walked in. By some mysterious "grapevine" someone had found and brought him. It seemed that they always had a way of finding anyone, even if they didn't know where he lived.

"I, Omar," he said, pointing to himself. "You know, Omar Sharif. I, Omar Sharif," and he laughed loudly, showing his healthy white teeth. Yes, yes, of course we knew Omar Sharif, and were delighted to have found someone who spoke a little English. Could Omar take us to a Gypsy settlement? "Tomorrow not. Tomorrow Omar works in tobacco fabrique. We go now." "O.K., Omar, we go now," we repeated, leaving the house. He bounded along beside us, gesticulating and laughing, with Osman following. As we were getting into the van, he announced: "Much Gypsies in Turkey. This all Gypsies here," pointing to the houses around us. Osman lived in a Gypsy suburb made up of small houses like his own, painted bright greens and blues. Looking around us, we saw that several other of the Izmir hills were dotted with colorful Gypsy dwellings. However, we told Omar that we wanted him to take us to some Gypsy village. "Good." He had understood. "I take you to Arapçiköy, fifty kilometers from Izmir."

On the way, we tried to learn as much as possible about the life of Gypsies in Turkey. We kept asking questions, but Omar was eager to hear from us where we were from and what we could tell him about Gypsies elsewhere.

"I never go from Turkey before. I thirty years. I want go Austria, Moses and Fatima there. Moses write me, and I go Austria. Turkey not good. Gypsy life in Turkey not good." He wanted to know how Gypsies lived in Yugoslavia, Germany and other places. He was very surprised to hear that his brothers could be found in India, Italy, France, the United States, all over the world. "Like me?" he asked. Yes, we assured him they were like him. He translated all this to Osman in great detail, excitedly waving his arms, and then said: "Osman ask, where Gypsies live most good?" We were at a loss: nobody had previously asked us this concrete and very understandable question and we hadn't thought about it. "In Sweden," we answered, not really sure it was true, but judging by the high general living standard... "Do Gypsies live good in Austria?" Osman wanted to know. "Yes, they live good," we said, catching ourselves using the same idiom, "those who work in factories." "Then all, whole family, go Austria when Moses send letter." We took this to mean that they would go if Moses managed to procure residence permits.

Several attempts to turn the conversation to Gypsies in Turkey were unsuccessful. To every question, Omar simply answered "Turkey not good," and continued cross-examining us.

Finally, after much talking, we arrived at the village called Arapçiköy: several dozen reed huts in a field, none of them enclosed by a courtyard. On the mud floors, covered with straw matting, whole families sat around on the ground. We noticed that there were no old people — in such conditions few live to an advanced age.

120

"India!" Omar shouted when we got out of the van. "See India!" None of us had the heart to tell him that this was even more depressing. Everywhere else outside of India we had noted that Gypsies lived better than in their country of origin. These, however, were quite tragic to behold. Confused by our visit, crushed by misery and poverty, they did not move from their places, or show any interest in us. Obviously half-starved, with sunken cheeks and lifeless eyes, they reminded us of pictures of Gypsies in Nazi camps during the war. Even the children did not mill around us or react to a camera. Nobody moved, nobody asked us anything, nobody even came to beg. "What do these unfortunates live on?" we asked Omar. "They pick cotton when people come ask. When people not come ask, they hungry." It was getting dark and we noticed that there were no lights in the village: neither tallow candles, nor oil lamps, nor even fires. When a Gypsy cannot light a fire because he has no

wood, then it is only a question of time, of low temperatures and the first snow, before his family is halved.

We started back for Izmir. With the light failing, we thought we had better call it a day. We told Omar we would like next day to visit the Gypsies in the hills, those whose women wear veils and men lead bears... "They not good," Omar said at once. Osman did not know them either, but Moses did. Maybe we should wait for Moses to come and go with him. Maybe we could do that some other time... But we were adamant: it had to be tomorrow, and we would pay whoever could take us there. Osman and Omar discussed this for a while in Romany, and we understood nothing of the conversation except for one word — Yugoslav.

"There one Gypsy, come from Yugoslavia, Macedonia, you know?

Group of Gypsies preparing for a festive meal. Engraving by J. Callot.

Maybe fifty years before," Omar told us. "He speak Yugoslav good, good man, Elmaz." He would find Elmaz and tell him to come to Osman's house next morning.

"Why not all of us go now, in the van, and tell him?" we suggested, thinking this would be a safer arrangement. "Not know where Elmaz live," Omar answered simply. "No problem, you come tomorrow, we find Elmaz. Elmaz be there, wait for you." "But how will you find him if you don't know where he lives?" we insisted. "Our brother know one Gypsy, Gypsy know Elmaz. This Gypsy know where Elmaz live. We find brother, brother find Gypsy, Gypsy find Elmaz." We couldn't help wondering how long this would take in a place like Izmir, built on as many hills as Rome. But they were doing it as a favor to us, just to please us... We parted from Omar and Osman at about 9 p.m., convinced that the next day would be wasted, that they would not locate Elmaz despite their best intentions...

At six in the morning, we left our hotel in search of Osman. It was a cold but sunny morning, and we felt optimistic — equipped with a tourist map of the city, we were bound to find the house easily. However, after almost an hour of roaming, we again ended up in a blind alley. "This area, my dear Zamur," I said, "can never have been visited by any of your architect colleagues." "Well, they wouldn't be able to do anything here anyway! The Gypsies themselves obviously build onto the houses, block the entrances to courtyards, enter through windows instead of doors, and have no address or house number," he replied. He suggested that we wait for him in the van, which was this time well and truly stuck. Half an hour later, Una and Richard, who had gone for a stroll, dashed back to say that Zamur was coming with Osman and another Gypsy, probably our "Yugoslav" guide. There was much laughing, kissing and hugging, to the amazement of the curious Gypsies who had gathered to see what these foreigners were doing in their alley with such a van.

"Brothers, I am Elmaz from Prilep, Macedonia. I am very happy, brothers, that I see you. Fifty years I didn't see Yugoslavs, now I see them." Short and plump, with a little moustache, nicely dressed for his meeting with us, hat in hand, he looked a real gentleman. "I am very happy, brothers. Fifty years I cry for my Macedonia. I didn't forget to speak. I tell my wife and children. I have two grown boys and three daughters. I have grandchildren, too. I say, we live in Turkey, but we are Yugoslav in the heart. We will go back there one day. I was eleven when my parents brought me here. Now they are dead. And my brothers and sisters no longer live. Only I am left. That is because I don't drink, I don't smoke, I don't bet on cockfights like these Turks do." Excited and happy, Elmaz poured out the story of his life, for, after all, we were compatriots and would listen to him. "There are many Gypsies from Yugoslavia here. Some stayed behind, didn't want to come with us. Much of my family and friends stayed behind. After the war one came from Prilep and said: Hitler killed many Gypsies there. What did Gypsies do to him, brothers? Nobody likes us Gypsies. Everyone chases us, wants us gone. And why, brother? What harm do we do? I will show you everything. Osman told me what you want. I know those Gypsies. I arrange everything and you photograph and have no problem. When everything is finished, we go back to my house, drink coffee, eat and talk. I tell my wife to make ready everything for guests, our compatriots, the best we have. You come to see my house, my family and my grandchildren..."

We let him talk, realizing it would be no use to ask him questions as yet. He simply had to pour out his heart to us, in his faltering and ungrammatical Serbo-Croatian, unload his feelings and memories. He told us of his youth. Although it can't have been rosy for Gypsies in Prilep at that time, he remembered it as something beautiful: all the bad memories had faded, and he talked as though it had been the happiest time of his life.

Driving towards Manissa, Elmaz's euphoria slowly abated. Now we could ask him questions. Listening to him talking about himself, his family and their life in Turkey, we were pleased to have found a guide like him. "I'm a different Gypsy from these here in Turkey. I didn't want to sell my two daughters, I gave them without money. I found them husbands as best I could, but I didn't take money for them. But you see, brothers, Osman for one daughter got 200,000 liras." We asked him why he hadn't taken any money for his daughters like the other Gypsies. "When I do that, she is his. He can beat her, and I won't let my children suffer. I can say, why do you beat her? You haven't paid for her, I can take her back if you beat her." We wanted to know why Osman had taken money, and Elmaz translated the question. After a long conversation, our guide told us: "He says his daughter costs him much. He must feed her, raise her, look after her, dress her. Every man needs a wife to have children, cook, work in the field and at home, so why not take money? He had to pay for his own wife also."

To change the subject, we asked Elmaz why the Gypsies we were heading for were so wild and distrustful. "They live away from the world," he answered. "The women wear black all their lives. Nobody sees their face, it is covered. The men have several wives — nobody even knows how many. They are afraid someone will come to their wives when they are away at the fair with their bears. But don't worry, I know their leader and I'll talk to him, explain everything to him, and you can photograph. If their leader gives permission, he will stay with us, and so nothing will happen to us." "And what," we asked, joking, "if some young lady falls in love with Zamur's beautiful red beard? Could he stay there with her in the village? Would the Gypsies accept him?" "Yes, they would, surely, if they see that he is true," Elmaz said, and Osman, to whom he had translated everything agreed.

"There have been such cases in Turkey," Osman claimed, joining in the conversation. "They say that ten years ago, one American disappeared in Izmir. His group looked everywhere for him, and didn't find him. The police thought somebody maybe killed him. Later, we heard that someone saw him with a group of traveling Gypsies, crossing into Iraq. There are cases like that, when Gadjas join Gypsies, but also when Gypsies disappear from the settlement. Sometimes it is because of a Gypsy girl, sometimes because they are tired of their life."

Osman also told us, through Elmaz, why strange things happen to people. "It is because when you are born, everything that will happen to you is written in a book. It must have said in that American's book about the Gypsy girl. And when you die, it says in the book where, how and when."

Then we changed the subject, asking Elmaz to tell us about the cock-fights. Were the birds used of a special breed? How much did a good fighting cock cost? How much could be won or lost? "I will take you tomorrow to see a cockfight. Tomorrow afternoon, in a café. My neighbor has fifteen birds, good fighters. They all fight, none of them run away. His birds are so good, they fight for two hours, until they kill the other. There is much blood: you must stand back not to get splattered. The birds must be the same weight. If one weighs a kilo, the other must weigh a kilo. To make him strong, the Gypsies feed him every day with two eggs, mixed with flour and nuts. He starts to fight when seven months old, and stops when he is two and a half. Both Gypsies and Turks bet, from 500 to 100,000 liras. A good fighting cock costs about 15,000 liras, the ordinary ones, for eating, 1,000. The birds train, like boxers: three, four times a week for ten minutes. Then when they grow up, they attack another cock as soon as they see him."

Chatting and laughing we passed Manissa, a pleasant little town some 30 miles from Izmir, and headed through an open valley towards Saruhanla. That day it was my turn to drive. At one moment, I noticed a group of cotton-pickers to our right. We needed such a shot for the book so I slowed down and stopped, as far right as possible.

"Zamur, photograph them before they notice us," I exclaimed. Already experienced in these matters, he leaped out of the van and took cover below the level of the road, followed by Elmaz, Osman and myself. Una and Richard decided to stay in the van and wait for our return. But the Gypsies had seen the vehicle stop, noticed Zamur with his cameras, and that was the signal for several of the men to head towards us armed with sticks, to stop us photographing their wives. Osman and Elmaz started a shouting-match with them, in Romany, but it was of no help. "Don't worry, brother," Elmaz said. "I'll see to it, just let him photograph them." Zamur was already doing just that, at top speed, without waiting for permission. Elmaz, Osman and I stayed together. We crossed the road to see if we could find a way of getting the van to the fields by some path below the road, and then returned, stopping at the edge of the asphalt. "We can't get through this way," Elmaz said. "We must go back." All three of us stepped out into the road together, Osman on my left, and Elmaz on my right. In the thousandth part of a second I sensed that something was approaching, felt the rush of air. I jumped back, instinctively grabbing out at Osman and Elmaz, and dragging Osman back with me. A small green truck bore down on us at great speed. Nobody could save Elmaz. Horrified, I saw him struck by the truck, fly through the air and fall into the ditch at the roadside. The first thing I felt was a terrible fear. Not of death, which I had barely escaped, but of the Turkish police and prisons. 'This is the end of the line,' I thought.

Hearing the shout that I let out, probably trying to warn Elmaz, Una, Richard and Zamur dashed towards us, afraid that it could have been me. In

76   With the first days of spring, Zoran Nikolić, his wife and children get their belongings together and set off with their bear on an eight-month tour of Yugoslavia. Marko, the bear, is allowed to ride on the cart with the family when he gets tired from walking. As winter approaches, they return to their winter quarters and tie up their bear until the following spring.

77   In the village of Idvor in Banat, near the Romanian border, a Gypsy drives a flock of geese to be plucked. In this lowland area of Yugoslavia, plucking geese and the sale of feathers and down is one of the Gypsies' traditional occupations. They usualy "hire" the geese from a peasant farmer, paying him up to 400 dinars per bird (c. 30 US cents). Geese are plucked three or four times a year (depending on the weather and how well-fed the birds are), between March and November. Gypsies in this part of Yugoslavia are estimated to pluck several million geese each year. (pp 126-7)

78   This Gypsy's job is airing the feathers by tossing them around in the fresh air, so they do not get mouldy. When dry, the down and feathers are classified according to quality. Of the four possible pluckings per year, the best are considered to be the second and the third, when the geese are "well covered". Finally the feathers are put into sacks and sold to the goose-feather trading stations, which frequently complain that Gypsies add sand to the sacks to make them heavier, and thus earn more money. The trading stations wash and dry the feathers and export them, free of sand, mostly to West Germany.

79 The plucking must be done fast and expertly, so that the goose suffers as little as possible. The pluckers must know the classification of the feathers: the down from the breast is the most sought-after, whilst the long feathers from the tail and wings are the least valuable. However, even these can be made use of, if plucked carefully. Should the peasant be dissatisfied with the way his geese have been handled, i.e. if they were injured in the plucking, the Gypsy responsible will not be given any geese to pluck the following year – a bad name spreads fast through the villages.

80 The "bald" geese recover very soon and are well fed by the peasant so as to be ready for the next plucking. In the winter the geese are not plucked, as they need a break and must keep their feathers as protection against the cold. The skilled Gypsy can make the equivalent of 10 dollars a day, which is considered very good earnings.

81

81   In Macedonia, where peppers are grown
on large plantations, the seasonal job of
picking them and packing them in sacks is
a Gypsy prerogative. The pay for a twelve-
hour day is about 8 dollars. Gypsies from
Macedonia travel to other parts of Yugoslavia
to work as seasonal labor: in Vojvodina, for
example, they are indispensable during
wheat and corn harvests. As we noticed,
Gypsies are a help to peasant farmers all
over the world, from India to Spain.

82   At a wedding in Macedonia, Gypsy musicians play a Macedonian folk dance similar to those performed in Greece. In this part of Yugoslavia, many peasants still live in the old patriarchal way and wear traditional dress. The instruments played by the Gypsies here are the zurla *and the drum, giving the music a Turkish, oriental character.*

83   Skopje, the capital of Macedonia, has an exceptionally large settlement of some 80,000 Gypsies called Šuto Orizari, which can be translated as "rice fields". This is probably the largest concentration of Gypsies anywhere in Europe. Known as Arlije, they have been living in the city as traders, gunsmiths, makers of saltpeter, gunpowder and rope, and musicians since the 17th century, when they accompanied Turkish armies. Skopje was then the crossroads of main trading routes to Greece and Turkey. It was in Šuto Orizari, built after the disastrous 1963 earthquake, that a much-publicized affair concerning the sale of Gypsy children originated.

84   The Ajdovica family built their home on
the outskirts of Sarajevo, the capital of
Bosnia-Herzegovina. They survive year after
year, one snowy winter after another,
without electricity or running water, beside
the city garbage dump. The average life
expectancy under such conditions is
estimated to be 28–30. This family lives by
begging, the recourse of those Gypsies who
can neither read nor write and have no skills
to earn a living.

85   Ismeta Redjaj, who lives in a Bosnian
village, agreed to talk to us, and even allowed
us to photograph her. "Let the whole world
see from your book how we Gypsies live.
Like we weren't people at all. There's no
work and no home for us, like there is for
others," she said. Ismeta's husband had gone
to the town to earn their bread by doing odd
jobs: chopping wood, unloading coal,
carrying sacks...

86

86   A funeral service in a Belgrade church – a Gypsy "guest worker" had died four days earlier in Germany but his numerous family wanted him to be buried in Belgrade. The service is conducted according to the Serbian Orthodox rites, to which the Gypsies have added their own customs: friends and relatives spend the previous night watching over the dead man. At midnight the table is laid for dinner, to which the men sit down while the women serve them. One place is left empty – the plate is piled with food, but nobody touches it: it is intended for the deceased. We wanted to photograph these customs, but were not permitted. After the funeral, the mourners go to the house of the deceased for dinner – we saw an ox turning on a spit in the courtyard. Dinner is served three times: twice for the guests, the third time for relatives and members of the household.

87　On the outskirts of the small town of Požarevac in Serbia, we met Živorad Jovanović. We were told that he had fought in the war, as a volunteer with the Partisans, and had lost a leg. When we arrived at his house, we found the whole family in mourning: they had just buried his son, Jovan, a young man of thirty, who had died of a heart-attack. "We Gypsies fought the Germans and did not let them just slaughter us without putting up any resistance. Many of us were killed, but some survived. In the Partisans there was a general feeling of brotherhood. It was lovely. After the war, little by little, we became Gypsies again."

88　Živorad Jovanović lives on his army disability pension. The other Gypsies in the settlement respect him as a man who showed that Gypsies, too, are worth something, and come to him for advice on how to solve problems with the authorities or attain their rights.

89

89 On Yugoslavia's Republic Day (November 29), we came upon this group of Gypsies playing to a few passers-by in the town of Požarevac. In the old Serbian Army the trumpeters were always Gypsies, being among the few soldiers with any knowledge of music. The military trumpet thus became one of the most common instruments played by Gypsies in Serbia. There is even a story which recounts how in the Balkan War (1912), during a battle against the Turks, one of the Gypsies sounded the Turkish retreat in the midst of battle, and thus helped the Serbs to win.

90   In Karaburma, a suburb of Belgrade,
a whole new Gypsy settlement has sprung
up in recent years with the arrival of Gypsies
who left the Kosovo region under pressure
from Albanians wanting an ethnically "pure"
province. This settlement, without electricity
or running water, is the poorest in Belgrade.
The municipal authorities are unable to
provide the inhabitants with better housing,
but neither can they take any action to
remove them from the site, as this would be
unconstitutional. Many of the Gypsies here
make their living by begging in the streets of
the capital.

91   In the Karaburma settlement we met
a Gypsy woman training a goat, an animal
that learns easily and is frequently used in
Gypsy shows. The scene brought to mind
another goat and its famous owner, the
Gypsy Esmeralda, in Victor Hugo's "The
Hunchback of Notre Dame".

*92   Skadarlija, the old Bohemian part of
Belgrade, is sometimes visited by bear-
tamers. The Gypsies brought this profession
with them from Turkey, and before that
India, where Gypsy bear-tamers can still be
seen. Ursari, in Romany ''bear leaders'',
occupy almost the lowest rung of the Gypsy
ladder, just above the beggars. There are
some 300 bears owned by Gypsies in the
vicinity of the Serbian town of Požarevac
alone. On national and religious holidays,
they tour villages and suburbs performing
their tricks. (pp 138-9)*

93 When not traveling, the bear Marko spends all his time tethered to a metal pole, scarcely able to move, out in the wind, rain and snow. He is fed with corn and stale bread. Unlike bears living in the wild, Marko does not hibernate: his need for food and contact with his owner keep him awake. We asked the owner why the animal had no shelter against the weather, and were told that it was very difficult and dangerous to approach a bear kept in an enclosed space – cases of an animal mauling its owner were not rare.

94 Zoran Nikolić controls his performing bear with a stick while his wife decorates the animal before the family set off in the spring on their travels around the country.

95   We photographed Zoran Nikolić and his family taking a rest on their way to Belgrade. Bear-trainers ''divide up'' the territory so as not to compete with one another. Their eight months of nomadic life entail constant work around the horses, the bear, and the covered cart in which they live with all their belongings. During the long and tiring journeys, little Janko and Rade, instead of a teddy bear, have a real one for company.

96   It is a Gypsy rule to find a suitable place to camp before sundown. The meal is cooked on an open fire – usually a chicken received as payment for some small service from a peasant, or found ''wandering all alone''. Then it is time for old Gypsy tales and legends. One tells of the origins of the bear: a Gypsy virgin, finding she had conceived, could not stand the shame and went to the river to drown herself. When she got there she heard a voice telling her not to do so, as she would give birth to a being from which all Gypsies would live: a bear.

97 Traveling through Bosnia, we came upon a group of Gypsies encamped near the river Neretva, just before the town of Mostar. When the weather is good and water is plentiful, the Gypsies may decide to do their spring cleaning. After having washed the laundry, collected firewood, cooked the meal and fed the children, the women still manage to find time to see to their menfolk. Usually lack of water and other factors do not permit them to pay much attention to their personal appearance and hygiene.

98   At the fairs still held in smaller places on a certain day of the month, most of the horse dealers are Gypsies. We visited the livestock market in Šid, some 60 miles west of Belgrade. Žare Tutela has been coming to this fair every fifteenth of the month for almost 50 years. He buys horses for the equivalent of about 250 dollars and sells them for 20–50 dollars more. Sometimes he even resells a horse at the fair at which he bought it, although that is quite a feat; most often the animals are sold to the knackers. When business has been concluded, he likes to have a drop of good old Serbian šljivovica (plum brandy). When we jokingly remarked that someone might cheat him when he gets drunk, Žare replied with a grin: "Have you even seen a Gypsy who doesn't drink or a Gypsy cheated by a Gadja?"

99 The cattle market has always been a social as well as commercial event – an occasion for families to meet, exchange news, discuss some future business, or the sale (wedding) of a daughter. It is important for Gypsies to be well informed about the goings-on in the area since this is the basis of their survival. Livestock markets and fairs are ideal for this, being visited by Gypsies from the whole region and not just one village.

100 Livestock markets where horses are traded are often visited by Italian buyers, equipped with the necessary permits, who frequently use Gypsies as a go-between with the peasants. They haggle over the price for them, and receive commission from both buyer and seller. Without the Gypsies, the prices would be higher, since many peasants are convinced that all foreigners are rich.

101–103 *A Gypsy wedding on the ourskirts of Belgrade. Many Yugoslav Gypsies working in West European countries return to their village to find a bride and get married in style, to show neighbours how well they have done abroad. The whole village is invited, food and drink abound, as many as three bands may be engaged – in short, no effort or expense is shared to impress the less prosperous.*

104 *The Gypsy "aristocracy", those working abroad, compete with one another in the size and lavish furnishing of the houses they build. Income from abroad has led to wide socio-economic differentiation among Gypsies in Yugoslavia. (p 148)*

a panic, I yelled at them to get back in and turn the van — we were going to make a run for the border before the police arrived. While they drove off towards a gas station up the road in order to turn, the truck-driver, who had managed to stop some fifty yards further on, ran over to me gesticulating wildly, obviously blaming me for the accident. I shoved him roughly away and scrambled down to Elmaz's side. He was, incredibly, still alive, but his head was a bloody mess, and his face hardly recognizable. ''Elmaz!'' I called to him. He tried to open his eyes. 'No, we can't leave him,' I thought. Zamur, up on the road above, sounded the horn to signal he was there and to hurry up. I turned and looked around. Only then did I notice Osman beside me, tearing at his hair in utter despair. I pointed to Elmaz's legs, and raised his shoulders. Osman understood my purpose immediately, and we carried him to the van.

''We can't leave him,'' I told Zamur. ''We must take him to he nearest hospital and let Osman take care of him and explain to the police. As soon as we've done that, we must make for the nearest border. On no account must we wait for the Turkish police.'' Zamur, mute with shock like the other three, stepped on the accelerator without a word. I sat by him, while Osman supported Elmaz's head so he wouldn't choke. I kept turning back to look at him, and the sight was ghastly: there was blood everywhere, pouring from his head onto the seat and floor of the van. Una and Richard sat in the back, trying not to look. Zamur never stopped sounding the horn, but this produced very little effect on the local drivers, who do it all the time. We seemed to stop dozens of times to ask for the hospital, wasting precious seconds, while Elmaz's breathing was becoming more and more erratic. When we finally reached the hospital courtyard and turned off the engine, there was total silence. We looked at him, and Una said: ''He's dead.''

We all clambered out of the van, as though trying to escape the fact. Then Osman and I returned, picked Elmaz up and carried him into the hospital. ''All we do is hand him over and get out,'' I kept repeating to myself. Osman would explain what had happened and how. Someone opened the door for us, and we entered the hall. The first thing I saw was the reception desk, and on it, in big letters, the sign: Police. I almost fainted from the shock — here was exactly what I had been afraid of, in the one place I hadn't expected to encounter it. I stood rooted to the spot, not knowing what to do. Should I put Elmaz down and run for it? But it was too late: several policemen were already approaching. Someone brought a trolley on which we gently laid the body. Then I dashed outside, suddenly remembering Una, and thrust an envelope with money into her hands, not realizing that it also contained my passport and driver's license.

''You and Richard get out of here as fast as you can! Take a taxi straight back to our hotel in Izmir and wait there. If we're not back by 3 p.m. (it was then about 9 a.m.), raise the alarm. Call the Embassy, or the Consulate. Do whatever you can.'' Seeing them disappear from the courtyard, I felt somewhat relieved — at least the young people were out of all this.

On my return to the hosipital, Zamur and I were taken by the police into an office, where Osman was already sitting, guarded by several soldiers with automatic rifles. ''This is it!'' I said to Zamur. ''What a place and way to end it all!'' ''We're not to blame,'' he kept repeating. ''It was the truck-driver's fault.'' But who on earth would ever find the man, last seen driving away at breakneck speed? Then I recalled the piece of paper Una had stuffed into my pocket just before leaving, saying something I hadn't grasped at the time. I reached for it. On it was written simply: 45 DU 990. She had had the presence of mind to take down the truck's number. No sooner had we sat down than a police photographer appeared and took photos of all three of us. 'This,' I thought, 'is really fast going.'

Soon an officer arrived and motioned us to follow him. With five or six policemen we went into the courtyard, where we stood for some time, unable to say anything for ourselves. Our English was of no use here, and we knew no Turkish, or even Romany. Osman was saying something, answering questions. Would he be able to explain that it wasn't our fault? I handed the piece of paper with the truck number to the officer. Realizing what it was, he immediately started giving orders: one policeman went over to a car and sent out a radio message, clearly ordering the driver to be brought in.

Then I suddenly thought of another way we could help ourselves. "Zamur, you're an architect and draw well. Do a diagram showing where we were and how it happened." In a few moments he had sketched a really professional-looking "reconstruction" of the accident, which I handed to the same officer. He seemed impressed — we had supplied him with two important pieces of evidence: the number of the hit-and-run driver, and an illustration of the accident. What next, we wondered? We were given a sign to follow, and led into a small building smelling strongly of formaldehyde: the morgue. In semi-darkness we made out a tiny figure on the floor, crumpled up, with one shoe missing — it was still in the van. Osman was pointing to him and obviously identifying the body. We nodded and confirmed: "Yes, this is Elmaz." Osman signed the form they handed him, and we were all led outside to a waiting police van with two policemen and a sergeant inside. With the siren howling, we returned to the scene of the accident.

When we reached the cotton fields after about half an hour's drive, all the Gypsies stopped picking and ran over to us. The police, their machine-guns at the ready, stopped them from approaching too close, but called one of the Gypsies over to question him. From his rapid and excited responses, we concluded that he must be accusing us. Maybe he was complaining about our taking photographs against their express wishes. The photographing of Gypsies was not likely to be very popular with the Turkish authorities, who might imagine it was done to blacken the reputation of the country and government. Suddenly we heard a commotion and saw the police dragging the driver out of a truck that had stopped some hundred yards away. Astonished, I recognized him as the man who had killed poor Elmaz: he had returned to the scene of the accident of his own accord, after coming to his senses or being advised to give himself up. After indicating the exact spot of the accident and the place in the ditch where Elmaz had lain bleeding, we were driven back to Manissa, past the hospital, to the outskirts of the town. We stopped in front of a large isolated building, with the sign "Turkish Gendarmerie" above the entrance and barred windows.

"They're taking us to prison," Zamur said, reading my thoughts. I tried hard to recall all the Turkish words I had ever known, but apart from sweetmeats — *rahat, lokum, baklava* — the only one that came to mind was *kismet*, fate, a word very appropriate to the situation we were in. Was it our destiny to end in prison, as Elmaz had ended, like so many Gypsies — in a ditch?

We were led into a waiting room where we were joined by a police sergeant and the truck-driver. He looked a sorry sight, as we probably did to him. Cracking his fingers and continually muttering, as though imploring Allah for help, he seemed resigned to his fate. He was then taken to a nearby office from which we heard the sound of a typewriter and concluded that he was making a statement. After a quarter of an hour, he was led past us into the basement, which was obviously the prison. As he walked past he looked at me, and his eyes seemed to say: 'Now I'm finished.' Then it was my turn. A police constable sat at the typewriter, while the sergeant questioned me standing up. He asked for my passport and driver's license. I took a piece of paper from the table and wrote out my name, place of birth and address in Yugoslavia, and the name of our hotel in Izmir. "Passport in hotel. Driver's license in the van, at the hospital," I prevaricated. I said that we were tourists — he appeared to understand that word at least. "We are staying six days in the hotel," I said, raising six fingers. All this time the policeman was typing away. Then the sergeant handed me the text — it was in Turkish and totally incomprehensible. If I refused to sign it could further complicate matters. If I did so, might I be signing my own death warrant? I signed, with grave misgivings.

They called Zamur next, and left me sitting with Osman. I was glad I had not been taken into the basement after questioning. Osman was weeping, wiping the tears away with the palm of his hand. How we, Gadjas, had changed his life since the previous afternoon! We had come bringing misery and misfortune. Then Zamur returned and Osman was taken in. He stayed twice as long as we did. When he was brought back, the three of us remained sitting there for another half hour, terrified — would they take us to the basement? Then the sergeant came, and gave us a sign to follow him towards the exit. "Hotel Hisar," he said and waved towards the courtyard gate. Unable to believe our good fortune, we hurried out. Maybe the last stop in our book on Gypsies would not, after all, be Manissa, Turkey. The policeman at the gate saluted us. We started running — anything to get away from that building — only stopping occasionally to wait for the plump Osman, who was quite out of breath. After covering about three miles, we found the van in the same place in the hospital courtyard. Zamur sat at the wheel, and we drove as fast as we could towards Izmir. After discussing our predicament we agreed that our safest course would be to get out of the country as fast as possible. Next day they might come to fetch us from the hotel and lock us up until the trial, or at any rate confiscate our passports.

We had about 100,000 Turkish liras on us. "Osman," we said, "take this money and give it to Elmaz's wife. You understand? Elmaz's wife." I looked at my watch — it was almost 4 p.m. The poor woman was getting supper ready for us. Instead of her husband bringing foreign guests, Osman would arrive alone. What could he say to her? *Kismet*. Gypsy destiny.

We said goodbye to Osman at the hotel. We hugged each other and kissed three times. We had never gone through this ritual with more sincerity...

Inside the hotel, we found Una frantic with worry, trying desperately to contact the Yugoslav Consulate by phone. Our bags packed and bill paid, the four of us made an unhurried exit, so that the people at the reception desk would not realize we were running away. When we were finally in the van, I said: "Straight to the border. What's the nearest one?" "Greece, about 650 kilometers away," answered Richard, who had sensibly been studying the map.

We drove at breakneck speed. Whenever we saw a police car or army truck on the lonely road, we imagined it was an ambush. Somewhere just before the Turkish border, we stopped to fill up the tank. Under the light of the lamps, Una suddenly noticed the blood on the seats, something we had overlooked. "Unless we wash this off, the first customs officer to flash a light into the van is going to have us all arrested," she said. We stopped at the roadside and she washed the blood off the seats and floor as best she could with a T-shirt and two bottles of mineral water.

At the border everyone seemed to be inside, dozing, as was quite natural in view of the time of night and the icy wind. The customs officers indicated the forms to be filled in, checked our passports and waved us through. Mixed feelings of relief and sadness overwhelmed us. The tragic death of a Gypsy on the roadside seemed somehow to symbolize the fate of his race, so often the victims, so often destined to meet a violent end.

Greece

Estimated number: 250–300,000
Date of arrival: 11th century
Main centers: Athens, Salonika, Serrai
Kilkis
Language: Romany
Religions: Orthodox, Moslem
Tribal groups: Rom, Handuria,
Kalpazaria

It took us one day by van to get from Belgrade to Salonika, the second largest city in Greece. We spent the chilly December evening in a warm tavern on the outskirts of the city, discussing our travel plans. Rajko reminded us of Grandfather Milan's story of how his family had come to Serbia from Greece some hundred years ago, and of the fact that it was the first European land in which Gypsies settled. They stayed here about two centuries before going on into the Balkans and western Europe.

Early in the 11th century they crossed the Dardanelles and Bosphorus and advanced, in smaller and larger groups, along the Roman Via Egnatia, bringing with them their customs, traditions, language and the crafts for which they are famed to this day. One of their largest settlements and transit stations was Modona (today Methoni), named Little Egypt because of the irrigation system which resembled that of the area surrounding the Nile. Hence the confusion in western Europe about the Gypsies' origins and name. "Greece has been a transit country for Gypsies crossing from Asia to Europe for the last ten centuries," Rajko told us.

Before going up to our rooms, we asked the hotel manager how to find Dendrapotamos the next morning. "What do you want to go there for?" he asked. "There are only Gypsies there." When told that was precisely why we wished to visit it, he was clearly taken aback, and the whole bar started discussing our folly and the Gypsies. All the customers seemed to have something to say about them, and most agreed that we should not go to Dendrapotamos unless we wanted to be cheated and robbed. The loudest of the guests, those who had had a drink too many, declared that all Gypsies should be rounded up and sent back to Turkey, where they had come from.

Very early next morning, before even the Gypsies had risen, we were making our way through the narrow alleys between the little blue-painted houses, built without any planning or permission. Apart from their color, they had something else in common — piles of scrap-iron in the courtyards and other waste collected in the streets of Salonika. Numerous scrawny, hungry-looking dogs roamed the alleys, since Gypsies do not tie up their animals: they are not used as guards, but serve only for company.

In front of one small house we met a muscular young man in an expensive leather jacket. It turned out that he spoke quite good English as well as Romany, and had come home from sea two days before to visit his parents. He had signed on with a ship three years earlier and had traveled all over the world. "I've seen the world, I've met Gypsies everywhere, but the Greek Gypsies, they're different. They have no destination; they are low down. I can speak Romany, but I don't want to. I don't want to be like them. None of my friends are Gypsies," he told us. The young man, who introduced himself as Nicholas Katheritis, took us to see the Gypsy elder, Yiannis, a well-dressed forty-year-old. In his neat little house, his pretty young wife peeled and sliced a plateful of various fruit and offered each of us in turn. Yiannis told us he was a small-time trader, like many Greek Gypsies. They go from market to market, and set up little stalls in the streets, selling lighters, miniature bottles of alcohol, cigarettes and anything else a passer-by might suddenly remember and need. He spends his spare time acting as an intermediary between the Gypsy Union and his brethren in the settlement, trying to get

152

them interested and active in the movement for improving their position in society. They want the authorities to open special schools in which Gypsy children would be taught in Romany, to have their own radio and television programs, a theater and newspapers, so that they can preserve their identity, which they are slowly losing. Nicholas is a good example of this tendency.

He told us that there were Gypsies all over Greece, but the largest concentrations were in Haghia Varvara in Athens, and in the towns lying between Salonika and the Turkish border, so we decided to look for them in the latter region.

Near the ruins of the ancient Macedonian city of Philippi we came across a settlement of some 2,000 Gypsies. Now in ruins, Philippi was raised by Philip II of Macedonia as a base from which to control the gold mines in the area. In 42 BC Brutus and Cassius were defeated by Octavian and Anthony

Traditional Gypsy costumes have been preserved by some of the Rom tribes, particularly by the Kalderash and, partly, the Spanish Gypsies (Kale). These are exclusively women's costumes with long, full skirts worn over several petticoats, in bright colors, predominantly red. Other tribes mostly adopted the dress of their environment or added many elements of this to their own.

under its walls. The city was twice visited by St. Paul, and his Epistle to the Philippians was addressed to converts there. Not having a local guide with us, we approached the settlement with care, leaving our cameras in the van. We were met by ''George'' Tramaris, who spoke a little English. Every so often he would take a swig from a whisky bottle, which would then be passed around. We dared not refuse for fear of upsetting the Gypsies and causing trouble, this being a test of friendship. Then Greek music started blaring from a van parked in the middle of the settlement, and the Gypsies rose and started dancing. We asked George what he did for a living. Instead of answering, he placed one chair atop another and started performing acrobatics. ''We're

a small group of performers," he told us. "We go to fairs and do acrobatics for the people. It doesn't pay well, so we do other things too: sell souvenirs and gold, smuggle whisky and other foreign drink. We're the Sicilian mafia here," he added with a grin. We also met Theo, aged 25. All the other inhabitants of the settlement were swarthy and black-haired, but he was fair. We asked him how this could be so. George answered for him: "Gypsy women are not the most faithful, and Gypsy husbands not the best in the world." Theo's sister approached us — she was fifteen and had been married for two years. While we stood around chatting, she swayed to the rhythm of the music, George caressing her occasionally. We gathered that her husband was sleeping off a drunken spree in their hut. "What else can we Gypsies do at night," George winked at us, "but drink and make love?" Others joined us, offering around food and drink.

Feeling we had been accepted, Zamur fetched his cameras and started taking photos. A swarm of tiny children milled around us, trying to pick our pockets. Zamur came over and complained that an expensive lens had been stolen, but we decided not to antagonize our hosts by mentioning that. We sat down at the tables and drank a beer each from the full crates they kept lugging up. They tried to persuade us to stay the night, as there was going to be a party, with lots of drink and music and hedgehog meat.

As they were just going to prepare it, we decided to watch. A Gypsy picked up a hedgehog, put a straw into its rectum and began blowing through it. The struggling animal started swelling, but the Gypsy blew steadily until it became like a balloon and stopped moving. We managed to avoid staying to supper by saying we were expected in Drama, but promised to return — feeling guilty as we had no intention of doing so.

Having met these Orthodox Gypsies, we now wanted to met some Moslems, so we went to Komotini. These Gypsies were different — not as hospitable and, like all Moslems, dangerous if they thought their women were threatened. As we walked through the settlement, keeping close together, the men glowered at us suspiciously. We encountered a group of giggling young women in baggy pantaloons who wanted their pictures taken. We

J. Callot:
"Beggars: frontispiece".
Etching.
(D. Ternois, "L'art de J. Callot",
Paris, 1962)

Drawing from the second half of the 18th century, representing a Gypsy from Czech Galanta playing on a wooden zither.

stopped, surprised at such a show of emancipation. A particularly beautiful girl arranged herself in a fetching pose and motioned that she was ready for Zamur to take photographs. When asked for her name, she called a young boy over to write it for her – she was illiterate. The boy wrote all the names down for us: Selia, Necibe, Muna, Sabia. "Sabia," the beautiful girl repeated, pointing to herself, and gave us the piece of paper. A Gypsy man who had been watching us at a distance now ran up, snatched the paper and started shouting angrily. He grabbed the pencil out of my hand and crossed the first three names off the list: two were his wives, the third his sister. He took them away, but left Sabia behind: she belonged to someone else, and he could look after his own. Jokingly, we asked her if she wanted to come along with us, pointing to the van. She nodded and moved toward the vehicle. But by then a group of men had gathered menacingly around us, and we bade her a hasty farewell. As we hurried away, Zamur said: "She really wanted to come along. She probably knows that a girl with her looks could live much better away from her Gypsy settlement."

We set off to look for the famous Via Egnatia, on the way discussing our cowardly and unchivalrous behaviour. We should, according to romantic literature, have taken Sabia with us, instead of leaving her to her furious husband, but this was real life, not a novel.

We came across a signpost marking the Egnatian Way, stopped the van and walked along it. Deserted and rather overgrown, it is now no more than a tourist attraction. It was a strange feeling to tread the stones of this once-great highway, traversed centuries ago by Macedonians, Greeks, Romans, Crusaders and pilgrims, monks, merchants and Gypsies. As we stood around, waiting for someone "photogenic" to pass, we heard the hum of traffic 150 yards away: life had moved elsewhere.

Yugoslavia

Estimated number: 800,000
First recorded mention: 1289
Main centers: Skopje, Belgrade
Language: Romany
Religions: Orthodox, Moslem
Tribal groups: Rom (Gurbeti, Arlije, Kalderash)

In the suburb of Belgrade called Karaburma, a Gypsy settlement sprang up, after 1980, unequaled in squalor by any of its predecessors on the outskirts of the capital. Soon after this, beggars, who at one time had almost vanished completely, reappeared on the streets. Women in pantaloons and headscarves, carrying toddlers and babies, poorly dressed for the cold and damp winter weather, would spend hours squatting on wet pavements, hoping to soften the hearts of passers-by by their misery.

In this settlement without electricity or running water, lying in a ravine which is flooded every spring, we came across 25-year-old Ibra Hodjica. He was suffering from some illness which had not been diagnosed as he had never been to a doctor. About a thousand of them, he said, had moved here from Kosovo, in southern Yugoslavia, which they had left not only because of poverty, but also because of pressure from the local Albanians who wanted an ethnically "pure" province. "We live on what our mothers and wives collect by begging in the streets. They can't do anything else as they're illiterate and speak no Serbian . . . The men also have no education and can not get jobs. In Kosovo we earned money as seasonal farm laborers. Now the Albanians do this work themselves and harvest with machines."

In Yugoslavia, with a Gypsy population of around 800,000, this is not a rare picture, although their standard of life varies considerably, depending on the area in which the Gypsies live. Those who have been settled for long periods are, to a certain extent, integrated in the economy of that region. Gypsies in Vojvodina have always had an easier life than those living in less fertile areas.

155

In the early spring we visited the little town of Požarevac, 70 miles south of Belgrade, knowing that semi-nomadic *Ursari* (Romany for bear-trainers) live in this area during the winter. The Gypsies brought this occupation with them from Turkey, where it is still carried on in villages throughout Anatolia, and before that, directly from India. The *Ursari* in the vicinity of Požarevac keep some 300 bears and perform with them throughout Serbia and Bosnia on state and church holidays. In a small, single-storey hut made of planks and mud we found Zoran Nikolić getting ready to leave on his eight-month annual tour with his family. All the time they are on the road the bear, Marko, is the only companion of his children, who play with their live teddy, but cautiously, as is necessary with outsize and dangerous playmates. Winter over, they were setting out with their cart drawn by a thin white nag (see back of jacket).

"When you see a bear dance," Rajko said, "accompanied by drums and tambourines, amusing the crowds who pay a few dinars to watch its antics, remember that this is never a pleasure for the bear, only pain." Marko, we were told, was captured at the age of two months. Gypsies know where she-bears hide and run great risks to snatch a cub from its mother, whom they drive out of her den with fire. Until it is about five months old the cub lives with the Gypsies, getting used to them. When it has grown a little and become stronger, it is time for training. Several Gypsies bring it to the ground, pierce its muzzle and place a ring in it. They also file its teeth to the gums to make it less dangerous. "This is extremely painful," Rajko told us. He had seen this done as a child. The bear is sick for about a month, and then it undergoes further torture. A rope is tied to the ring and the free end thrown over a branch and pulled taut, forcing the bear to raise its head. Its owner then beats the animal's front paws, and sometimes even cuts or burns them. The bear tries to avoid the pain by standing on its hind legs. As this is done to the accompaniment of drums and tambourines, every time it hears the noise it associates it with pain and rises. Similar methods are used to teach it to turn around in circles, take the Gypsy's hat off, collect money, and perform other tricks. During the 30–35 years of its life with the Gypsies, it eats nothing but corn and stale bread, and when not dancing, is tethered to an iron pole, unable to move around, spending its days and nights outside in all weathers. *Ursari* are considered by other Gypsies superior only to beggars.

In the Šuto Orizari settlement in Skopje, the capital of Macedonia, there are some 80,000 Gypsies, known as Arlije, making this the largest concentration of Gypsies in any one settlement in Europe. It grew particularly fast after the catastrophic earthquake which destroyed half of Skopje in 1963. Gypsies from all the settlements in the town itself and from all over Macedonia occupied the caravans, huts and other temporary prefabricated accommodation sent to Skopje as first aid, and added on to them, using the building material strewn all over the city.

When they saw us approaching with our cameras, they became threatening and started swearing at us. Rajko explained that this was probably because, in the last two years, the press and the police had become very interested in the selling of Gypsy children as thieves, pickpockets and beggars in Italy, France and other west European countries. A powerful young man of thirty or so approached us. "What do you want here?" he asked us fiercely. "You interested in Gypsies? There are no Gypsies here, only Macedonians. You have a permit to photograph? You get it from the police or we break your cameras." Fortunately, Rajko had an acquaintance in the settlement, Redžep, who was involved in the movement for the advancement of Gypsies and proved very kind and helpful. He confirmed that our encounter with the threatening young man was a consequence of the bad publicity given the settlement in the press. "Apart from which," Redžep said, "his authority

105   In Sibiu we were greeted by this Gypsy woman with the traditional "Dobroy", meaning "Welcome". Although the authorities deny the existence of Gypsies in Romania, there are estimated to be as many as one million living there at present. About 40% of them still speak Romany. The others have forgotten the language, a result of centuries of slavery, from which they were not freed until 1851.

106 Ion Andrescu, a smith living in Sibiu, also has a Romany name, Angar, meaning "charcoal", a part of every smith's daily work. The long hair and beard is a distinguishing tribal feature, brought from India over 600 years ago, and related to the belief that a man's strength resides in the hair. (pp 158-9)

107 Like Romanian peasant houses, Ion's home is full of embroidered articles and icons of the Orthodox Church, to which the Gypsies in Romania belong. Outside of India, Gypsies have always been compelled to live a double life: the one shaped by their distant past, the other by the reality and way of life of their host country. (pp 160-1)

108 Ion makes bread tins, cauldrons and other cooking utensils in a little shed in the winter, and in the courtyard of his house when the weather permits. These he sells illegally at the open-air market to peasants: the authorities do not look kindly upon this kind of trade. The craft of working metal, which Ion learnt from his father, has been handed down from father to son for hundreds of years.

109 The life of a Gypsy family revolves around the fire. The women wear long skirts, these being more practical for sitting around the hearth and covering their legs, which are not supposed to be revealed. Apart from this, they provide additional warmth at night.

110 These Gypsy women in Sibiu obviously also have some Romanian blood, their heritage from the period of slavery, when the owner had the right to have his pleasure with any Gypsy woman who took his fancy, as well as to offer her to his male guests. Here we see the women in their traditional costume, getting ready to take part in a pilgrimage to Petrinyants, in honor of the Virgin Mary.

1

111   Icons, and also a silver goblet, the Gypsies' greatest wealth and status symbol, are carried on pilgrimages. We were not permitted to photograph the goblet, as they claimed that it was sacred. On such occasions the women don all their jewelry as they will meet many others and wish to appear at their finest.

118   In this village in the Sibiu area we were warmly welcomed on our first visit, cut short by the police, who objected to our photography. On our second trip, the reception was not so friendly – we were even greeted with stones.

119   The earliest mention of Gypsies' arrival in Hungary dates from 1417, before the advance of the Turks. Being skilled in crafts which were in demand, they were well received by the king, Mathias Corvinus (1458–1490), and settled near larger towns, especially around Hermannstadt. Illustrated: a Gypsy girl and her brother in Dravaszabolc.

126   In the USSR we had to make do with photographing state-organized Gypsy bands in orchestras and theatres. There are no street performers, we were told, and Gypsy music, a remnant of decadent bourgeois society, is now reserved in Moscow almost exclusively for foreign tourists. One of these Gypsy floor shows takes place every evening in the Mezhdunarodnaya Hotel in Moscow.

127   Although the Soviet authorities have virtually put a stop to their wanderings by assigning them to regular jobs, Gypsies still gravitate towards their traditional occupations, like Vanya in the picture, who looks after the horses on a cooperative in Moldavia.

is probably based on collaboration with the police. In every Gypsy village the police have an informer who doesn't hide this fact, but uses it to gain authority among the Gypsies. He imposes himself on them and wants them to be afraid of him."

Most of the inhabitants of the settlement, Redžep told us, earn their living honestly by traditional Gypsy crafts or working in factories, and do not draw attention to themselves, but some have become smugglers, cashing in on occasional shortages of certain goods on the market. They cross into Italy and Austria, legally or otherwise, and bring back various merchandise which they sell through their connections. The children sold abroad had most probably crossed the border illegally, for Gypsies know exactly where and how to avoid patrols. They can, of course, obtain a passport in a few days, just like anyone else, if only they apply, but this requires forms to be filled in, photographs taken, taxes paid, and they have neither the time, the inclination, nor the patience for this. They are impulsive and rarely plan anything in advance: an idea simply comes up during some talk and the next day they are on their way.

Redžep explained to us the so-called sale of children: "Gypsies don't see these things like westerners. Every Gypsy works, contributes... When a grown Gypsy goes to Italy, as many do, he says to his neighbor or relative: 'Give me that child to take with me so that it can earn something and learn something, since you're only feeding it for nothing here.' The parent answers: 'Take it, but bring it back, and let it bring us something, too.' So the Gypsy has one mouth less to feed and even earns something."

On our return to Belgrade Rajko invited us to go to his cousin in Mladenovac who was celebrating his son's departure to do his military service – an old Serbian custom. In the yard in front of the house, a tent which could seat about 400 had been raised, with long trestle tables and benches inside. Above the central table stood a flag and a portrait of President Tito. There was a great babble of voices as the Gypsies kept rising from the tables and calling to friends and neighbors. Relatives had come to the celebration by car from Austria, Italy, Germany, France... There were many young people, the girls in long dresses of every color, the young men in black leather jackets. In the center of the tent – a band and a Gypsy singer, their performance amplified by huge loudspeakers. We tried to talk to the Gypsies, but could not make ourselves heard above the din, and had to go outside to get answers to our questions. The father of the young recruit was extremely excited. Almost half his relatives live in Austria, returning for holidays and such celebrations, bringing money, building houses in the village, competing as to whose will be larger and more comfortable... Work abroad has led to wide socio-economic differentiation among Gypsies in Yugoslavia: while some can afford to entertain 400 people, others, in the same village, beg for their living. When we returned to the tent, our host shifted some of his guests to seat us. Nobody complained as we were *Gadjas* (strangers) who had come with Rajko, a person they all knew well. Enormous quantities of food and drink were being consumed. Soon the guests started producing bundles of notes and calling the musicians to their tables. As the singer could not be everywhere at once, the Gypsies began raising their offers, competing for the privilege of having music at their table. They spared no expense that evening – they wanted to drink, sing and forget the hardships and humiliation endured to get their money. We asked the leather-clad youths where they worked in Austria, and they mostly answered in the municipal services, meaning garbage-removal, street-cleaning...

About midnight the music stopped and the Gypsy sitting next to the young recruit, his godfather, stood up and announced that now the money and gifts would be handed over. The future soldier also rose – he was eighteen, had been married for three years and had two children. First he presented his godfather with a shirt and tie. Then the latter announced over the microphone the sums which the young man had received. This provoked real competition among the guests, as nobody wanted to give less than his neighbor. On hearing their name announced, already rather drunk, they often increased the amount: the gift was presented in German marks, French francs, Austrian schillings ... Only very rarely did one of this Gypsy elite mention the Yugoslav currency – the dinar. And so it went on until dawn.

Zamur's comment, when we were leaving, was: "This celebration is not a truly happy occasion. It's even rather sad. Is there any real Gypsy merrymaking?"

"Yes," Rajko answered, "in story books."

Romania

Estimated number: 1,000,000
Date of arrival: 14th century
Main centers: Bucharest, Brașov, Timișoara
Language: Romany
Religion: Orthodox
Tribal groups: Rom (Aurari, Kalderash, Lautan)

When we were supposed to set off for Romania, to visit the Gypsies and see how they live, we approached the Romanian Embassy in Belgrade for permission. As we would be carrying very expensive photographic equipment and driving off the beaten tourist tracks, Rajko thought it wiser to travel with the blessing of the Romanian authorities. Our letter to the Embassy explaining the reason for our visit was typed on the official notepaper of the Romani Union, the world union of Gypsies, of which Rajko was Secretary-General. "They're bound to be impressed by the letterhead and the signature of the Secretary-General of a world organization, and won't be able to refuse us," Rajko said.

Having waited patiently for fifteen days and received no answer, Rajko phoned the cultural attaché of the Embassy, explained the situation, and was aksed to call back in an hour's time. This he did, and was promptly informed: "There are no Gypsies in Romania and, in consequence, we see no reason to give you permission or even any purpose in your proposed trip." Well, what now? Without Romania our book would lose a great deal. This was the only country in Europe in which slavery existed until 1851, the slaves being Gypsies. During World War II, although Romania was not occupied by the Germans, over 35,000 Gypsies were executed. According to the Romanian census of 1977, 230,000 persons declared themselves as Gypsies. Since many had good reason not to do so, their true number was estimated at over a million. So where had they all disappeared? We were obviously going to have to find out the answer for ourselves, so we decided to travel to Romania as tourists. "Let's go to Timișoara first," Rajko suggested. "We'll be met there by friends, Ioan Cioaba, the Gypsy Voivoda – leader – of the Sibiu region, and Nikolo Gherghiu from Bucharest. We can discuss our problem with them and try to find a solution. The important thing is not to take any cameras with us on this first trip, or they may well be impounded." Zamur, the owner of the expensive cameras, wholeheartedly agreed.

The following day we drove to the border crossing in a small Renault 4, so as not to attract attention, and as the cold January morning was hardly conducive to tourism, we crossed without the usual wait.

At Timișoara railway station, the agreed meeting place, Rajko soon found his friends. Short and plump, wearing a shiny leather jacket and a fur cap, the Gypsy Voivoda, Ioan Cioaba, approached us first and shook hands with Rajko for a long time, obviously delighted to see him. Then he greeted us, asking Rajko whether I, too, was a Gypsy – Zamur's fair hair and reddish beard could not fool anyone. Then Nikolo came across to greet us: slim, exceptionally tall for a Gypsy, in a dark coat and fur hat, elegant and reserved, he looked more like a Voivoda than Ioan did. After greeting Rajko in Romany, he spoke to us in excellent English: "Unfortunately, we'll all have to pile into your car. I couldn't come in mine — two months ago owners of private cars were forbidden to drive their vehicles until further notice. One day it snowed heavily, and it was announced that, in the interest of road safety, everyone was to leave his car where it was at that time. There's no more snow on the roads, but the ban has not been lifted. Most of us feel that it was because of the gas shortage."

While driving along we explained why we were in Romania. They were both enthusiastic about the idea of a book on Gypsies of the world, and agreed to help us meet and photograph their compatriots. Rajko mentioned the name of a Gypsy settlement in which, he had been told, there were several thousand inhabitants. After stopping several passers-by and much driving around in circles, we got to the site — but all we found was some straw, a few planks and tin cans, old clothes and fresh traces of bulldozing. Where were they? What had happened to them? We waited for someone to pass, and got Nikolo to find out. He was told that a few days before police cars and bulldozers had arrived, and in a short time everything had been razed to the ground. The police had informed the curious that the Gypsies would be moved to a new, more sanitary settlement, specially built for them, as this place had been an eyesore for ages.

"We are only two or three days too late," said Ioan, trying to console us. He remembered that he had the address of a Gypsy who lived on the opposite side of town, so we squeezed into the Renault again and set off for the house. We found a young man, Mirce, remarkable for his complete set of gold teeth, with his wife and two children, sitting on a large old-fashioned bed in quite a spacious but freezing cold room. They were wearing sheepskin coats and fur caps. Apart from the bed there was only an oil heater in the room, and it was not working. We were told that they could not heat the room because of the shortage of oil.

Our arrival had been noticed, and soon there were some twenty Gypsy neighbors sitting with us in the room which measured about ten feet by fifteen. "This is why Gypsies can never be good conspirators," laughed Nikolo. "There can be no secrets among them. They all want to take part in everything, and share both friends and enemies."

The Gypsies squatted on the floor. They all wore sheepskin coats and fur caps, except for one with a wide-brimmed felt hat. On every finger he wore a heavy gold ring, and his teeth were capped with gold, as is the custom among Gypsies in Romania. We had noted a similar one in India among the Banjara tribe, except that there they had pieces of gold inlaid in healthy teeth, which was probably easier than capping them completely. Exuding an air of prosperity, this man did not seem afraid of displaying his wealth — not advisable in Romania for anyone to do, let alone a Gypsy. When we asked why he wore a hat instead of a fur cap like the rest, several Gypsies answered at the same time: "He spent four years in France and just came back." What about other Romanian Gypsies, we wanted to know — did they go abroad to work as well? Those who were clever and "knew how to manage things". After some prompting, we found out that the phrase meant being able to fool the authorities. This was promptly illustrated by the story of some Gypsies who had exploited the political situation and now lived "prosperously" abroad. This group had read in the papers that exit visas had been granted to some Romanian citizens of the ethnic German minority, which had been living in Romania for generations, so that they might visit their country of origin. This was because a high German government official was scheduled to visit until his wife had cooked a chicken. "It will be ready soon, by the time we've finished off the bottle," he told us. Remembering Timişoara, we teased him that he must have got hold of heating oil because he was one of the privileged. "No, I have wood. If you have money, you can get anything." We made a tour of the house, which was new and spacious. There was a black-and-white television and some other electrical goods we had not expected to see. Obviously he was quite well off. We asked him to explain what his title of Voivoda actually meant. "There used to be many Voivodas," he told us. "Every larger group of Gypsies had its own. The Romanians had them, and so did we, Gypsies. Now there's neither the one kind nor the other. I'm the only Gypsy Voivoda left who is acknowledged by the authorities. My Gypsies make pots and pans, collect scrap-iron and, through me, work for the government. I'm their representative. Voivoda is an inherited title. They listen to me and obey me; they know I want to help them, that I don't want to take anything that is theirs. When they get into trouble, quarrel or fight, they come to me for advice. Why go to court, when I can help them solve their problems in a brotherly way?"

As he talked, he kept looking outside to see what Zamur was doing. "Let him photograph my Gypsies as much as he likes. In all these little houses around live relatives of mine, and while you're guests in my home, nothing can happen to him and nobody can complain!" He kept topping up our glasses the moment we put them down, even if they were still half-full. So we would not end up under the table, we suggested that while the chicken was being cooked, we should go to the Leiash village. "Whatever you wish," Ioan cheerfully agreed.

We piled into our van and half an hour later reached the village of Arpasul near Braşov, about twenty-five gaily-painted little houses clustered together near a stream. These are inhabited by the long-haired smiths whose ancestors had brought their craft and cult with them from India. When we entered the first courtyard, it was as though a circus had arrived. Everyone

J. Callot:
"Beggars: the cripple".
Etching.
(D. Ternois, "L'art de J. Callot",
Paris, 1962)

rushed to greet us, everyone wanted to have their photo taken. Amidst the laughter, jokes and handshakes, we noticed a solitary Gypsy mount a horse and ride off. He was the only one not to greet us on our arrival. Then we were offered brandy again, and glasses were handed round. Zamur came over to take another camera from the bag Rajko and I were looking after: "This will be wonderful material – we've certainly got off to a great start, knock on wood!" Shortly after this exchange, a police car came speeding up to the village, followed by the rider. The police asked for all our photographic equipment, and we had no choice but to hand it over. The attitude of the Gypsies towards us immediately changed, but that was only their method of self-preservation, the principle being – have nothing to do with those out of favor with the authorities . . .

The police ordered us into the van and took Ioan in their own car, probably so we would have no chance to cook up a story together. They signaled us to follow them. The three of us were seriously worried: we had been naive to think we would pass unnoticed with all that equipment at the frontier. Zamur, convinced it would be confiscated, mourned his cameras. Anxious and downcast, we arrived at a police station. Would we end up in prison? What should we say when questioned? The policemen got out of their car and Voivoda Ioan followed them, looking very dejected, having realized that brandy and high spirits had led him unwisely to take us to the village to photograph the Gypsies. "He'll get out of it all right," Rajko said. "He must be on good terms with them – he has a lot more than the other Gypsies, and travels abroad while others can't get visas." We were sorry we had gotten him into trouble, but there was no point thinking about that at this stage. We made to get out of the van, but were motioned to wait inside: we were not even able to relieve ourselves after all the brandy we had drunk! Hours dragged by. It was already dark when finally, in the light of the lamp above the station door, we saw the policemen emerge with our equipment. "Here, they said you're to take these and go back to Yugoslavia, and that you mustn't take any more photographs," Voivoda Ioan reported. Zamur checked that all the cameras and films were there. If the film had not been exposed, all might yet turn out well.

On our return journey, we wondered what would happen to Ioan. We decided to write him a letter, telephone, ask Nikolo about him. Then we turned to business. We decided that we still needed more material from Romania, especially from the village where the police had picked us up. Well, we should have to go back again.

* * *

Two weeks later, having learned that Ioan was at liberty, we set off for Romania a third time, carrying only a small Laica camera. When we appeared at Ioan's house, we met, understandably, with a much cooler reception, and soon set off for the village alone, since Ioan prudently refused to accompany us. The moment the villagers saw us, they started throwing stones: quite a different welcome from the last time. "This lot aren't joking," we decided, and drove on in the direction of Bucharest. Encountering Gypsies on the way, we took photos almost without getting out of the van until we came upon a camp. In a moment we had forgotten about the risks. We went over to the Gypsies, talked to them, took pictures and left, this time without an escort.

Several months later we made enquiries about Ioan, and were dismayed to hear that he was in prison. We may find out some day whether the Voivoda's fall from grace had anything to do with our visit.

Estimated number: 600–800,000
First recorded mention: 1417
Main centers: Budapest, Szeged, Debrecen
Language: Romany
Religion: Catholic
Tribal groups: Rom, Vlahura

Dravaszabolc is a typical village of the Hungarian plain: the houses, edging long straight roads, have large gardens and yards extending behind them and ending in fields. The farmland, formerly privately owned, became the communal property of the co-operative after World War II. Outside the village, in a gully beside the river Drava, lies a settlement raised by Gypsies some hundred years ago. Having put down roots here, they worked as village servants, seasonal field-laborers and blacksmiths, mended pots and pans, and wove baskets from the reeds and osiers growing by the river.

After the war, the Hungarian government, inspired by Soviet efforts, attempted to turn them all into farmers on the collective land, the idea being that all members of society, even Gypsies, should be engaged in organized productive work. Time passed, but the Gypsies continued to resist the government policy of assimilation designed to transform them into "decent Hungarian citizens": they made vain attempts to escape and sabotaged their work in every possible way to avoid a kind of life to which they were not accustomed. Eventually the government realized the futility of trying to integrate the Gypsies and left them to their own devices, although not always and everywhere...

Loaded with coffee, chocolate and other tokens of our goodwill, we were taken to Dravaszabolc by Ferenc Miklos, our Hungarian connection. He handed these gifts to the first Gypsies we came across in the village, and then we entered the settlement. "These are proof that you come in friendship," he said. "Only friends bring presents, while enemies come with whips." The Gypsies spoke Hungarian interspersed with only a few Romany words when referring to something that was typically theirs, the Gypsy life and customs. Some 40% of Hungarian Gypsies speak no Romany at all, we were told, and the rest use a great many Hungarian words.

A tall, thin Gypsy called Jànos invited us to his home, a daub and wattle structure like all the others in the village, and very sparsely furnished. Most of the Gypsies here, Jànos told us, earn their living by helping on the collective farm at harvesting time, for which they are paid in wheat and other produce. For the rest of the year, they weave baskets, collect old things which they sell at fairs, and smuggle goods. "We cross into Yugoslavia," he told us, "and give our Gypsies on the Yugoslav side of the border forints for dinars and other things." What happened if they were caught, we asked. "Oh, they lock us up for ten days, and let us go when we promise not to do it again. But they know, and we know, that our promise means nothing and that we'll soon be back. This has been going on, this game of cat and mouse, for as long as anyone can remember."

The Gypsies were not the only ones to notice our arrival in the village: our van with a foreign number-plate and the many cameras attracted the attention of those who keep an eye on the "unreliable" Gypsies. A Hungarian rode up on a motorbike and asked what we wanted with the Gypsies. We explained who we were and the purpose of our visit. "Why don't you take pictures of your Gypsies in Yugoslavia – you have more than we do," he said, "instead of coming here to put Hungary to shame?" "How can our photographing Gypsies do that?" we asked. "Because they are lazy layabouts and thieves who live off society, the working people. They're trouble-makers," he declared, adding quite a few other insults.

Ferenc explained that this was a man from the village who was assigned to check up on the Gypsies. He left as suddenly as he had appeared, and we went on taking photographs and chatting. Some twenty minutes later we saw two armed soldiers approaching us, our "official" following them slowly on

128 Gypsies arrived in Italy in 1422. After several years of wandering, they were forced to leave it, hounded by the clergy, but returned several decades later to continue their nomadic existence on Italian soil to this very day. Although after World War II the automobile replaced the horse, Gypsies nevertheless remained sentimentally attached to their four-legged friends. This is also shown by the greeting "May your horses live long", meaning "May you have a happy life". Illustrated: little Carlo from Udine.

129   In Pescara Gypsies keep horses for the trotting races so popular in Italy. Vittorio spends most of his time with his horse, which has repaid this care by winning several races. These beautifully groomed animals have replaced, in Pescara, the underfed, bony nags which could be seen in the area, drawing heavy caravans, until a decade ago.

131   This old type of wooden caravan is becoming rare. Gypsies, like tourists, have changed to the lighter, easily maneuverable, plastic ones.

130 Proud of their horses, the Gypsies in Pescara take every opportunity to gallop through the town streets, driving the traffic cops to despair.

132 The interior of a Gypsy caravan sometimes compares favorably even with the homes of the most particular Italian housewives. More often, however, the opposite is the case.

133 A
horse-tr
they are
living by
fairs. Th
Gypsies
to conju
tales, so
mytholo

137   Since several generations live together in the traditional Gypsy family, feeding all the members is an onerous task. Fortunately, there are always plenty of women around willing to lend ''Mama'' a hand when needed, as here at the Paolo Veronese camp in Turin.

138, 139 In the suburbs of Turin we visited the Paolo Veronese camp, inhabited by Sinti from Piedmont and Lombardy. This group of Gypsies waited, chatting in the open air, opposite the suburban skyscrapers, for "Mama" to prepare their meal. The commune of Turin permitted the forming of six temporary camps, on condition that the total number of Gypsies living in them does not exceed 3,000. The camps have the status of temporary dwellings, which means, in practice, that they can be moved elsewhere or razed to the ground should such action be considered necessary.

140 This little girl is holding an Easter egg, for Gypsies also celebrate the feasts of their host country in addition to their own. When they move from one country to another, they adopt the language and customs of their new host – a necessity of the Gypsy way of life.

141 In Alberobello, against a background of picturesque trulli (houses with conical slate roofs), Rajko Djurić chats about Gypsies with one of the locals. He was told that they sell wrought-iron articles at the market, mostly to tourists visiting this quaint little town in the south of Italy.

*146–149 The funeral of a Gypsy horse-
trader in Udine is according to the rites of the
Catholic Church, but the customs of his
people are also observed. The body of the
deceased is displayed in his home and
spends the night there. During this time no
animal may enter, lest the spirit of the dead
man should take possession of it. All mirrors
must be covered up, so that his soul will not
be trapped inside the house. Measures are
also taken to prevent him from becoming
a vampire. On the graves of horse-traders it
is not unusual to raise figures of their means
of livelihood.*

150 In Turin the authorities designated a place for Yugoslav Gypsies, who number about 10,000 in Italy. In this camp, Strada Druento, there are some 2,000 of them. Their head is Šefkija Salkanović from Sarajevo, Bosnia. His "insignia" were designed by him and made by his wife. The wheel, he explained, represents the eternal movement of his brothers from India to the end of the world; red is the Gypsy color, blue stands for the sky, while green is for the grass on which they spend most of their lives.

151 The Gypsy "committee" in this settlement consists of Šefkija and "delegates" whom the Gypsies chose to represent them and their interests. The delegates, chosen so that each extended family is represented, jointly settle all disputes that arise within the camp or with the authorities. Šefkija meets with his people daily to decide the plan of action for that day. Some sell wrought-iron or copper articles, some tell fortunes, some collect second-hand and discarded goods, and some, "to tell the truth", as Šefkija admits, will spend their day in one of the oldest of all Gypsy pursuits – theft.

152 Women belonging to the "beggars' group" in the camp are getting ready to go into Turin, where they will spend the whole day going from house to house or stopping passers-by on the street asking for money. Their individual daily "take" sometimes amounts to over 100,000 liras.

153　In the settlement we found Šefkija's children watching Japanese cartoons on Italian television, as they do all day long. Šefkija claims this is ''very good'' as it keeps them off the streets and from getting knocked down by the cars which speed past the camp. The children were born in Italy and, apart from Romany, also speak Italian. The parents still use Serbo-Croatian, but increasingly rarely.

154 *These Gypsy women are amusing themselves telling fortunes by "reading" the coffee grounds left at the bottom of each cup of Turkish coffee. When asked whether they believed in all that, they answered that it was a good way to practice what they would say to the Italian* signoras.

155 *Fikreta sets off with her baby to spend the day begging for alms outside a church. After leaving mass or confession, people are usually in a more charitable mood, and are further moved to generosity by the sight of the infant. Although circumstances may oblige them to exploit their children in this manner, Gypsy mothers, she assured us, take good care that the infants are well wrapped up.*

156, 157   Now that they are mostly motorized, it is no problem for the Turin Gypsies to pop over to Milan where, in the square in front of the cathedral, there are always plenty of people interested in the services of Gypsy fortune-tellers.

With a vocabulary of about fifty words, these Gypsy women from Bosnia, Yugoslavia, will tell the signoras of children that will be conceived, but only by those who wish for them, about husbands who will return or those to come, of tall dark strangers, messages and money – in short, just about

anything most of us would like to hear. "I can tell by the face what I should say," Nusrija explained to us. "I only ever speak of good news, never of the bad, as there is no fixed price for fortune-telling and people pay as much as they want to. Nobody gives money for bad news."

158

158   At dusk on a wintry day all the Gypsies from the Strada Druento camp have returned. Apart from the goods "bought" in the supermarket, sometimes they also bring a cart or two, in case it should come in handy for some purpose the shopkeepers never envisaged. It happens, however, that a certain number end the day in a cell: about twenty Gypsies from the camp were in prison when we were there. Their comrades visit them regularly, bringing them tobacco and other little luxuries, until their sentence has been served.

159   Little Sophia, like most other Gypsy children, is often left to her own devices while her mother is in the city. Happily, there are always playmates to be found.

159

his motorbike. Having learned something from our Romanian experience, we piled into our van and left for Budapest. "Will we be stopped on the way?" we asked Ferenc. "I don't think so," he answered. "They probably only wanted to frighten you and chase you away. The authorities don't like foreigners mixing with the Gypsies and visiting their villages. When they write about us, it looks like a criticism of Hungarian society, because it hasn't managed to assimilate us and turn us into Hungarians. At one time there was talk that if we resisted assimilation, they intended to sterilize all Gypsy women, like they tried to do in Czechoslovakia, but they gave up that idea."

In Budapest we visited two famous restaurants, Matyàs Pince and Citadela. As in many other Hungarian restaurants, Gypsy musicians were playing. The music was Hungarian, but it had the special quality imparted, as Franz Liszt noted, by the passion and temperament of Gypsy musicians. We asked the manager for permission to photograph, explaining that we were doing an article on Hungarian Gypsy musicians, and he agreed. However, no member of the orchestra would admit to his Gypsy origin: they were not there because they were Gypsies, they protested, but because they were first-class musicians. "When a Gypsy makes it in Hungary," Ferenc told us, "he turns away from his brethren because connections with them might be harmful to his career. This is because Gypsies are still generally regarded as second-class citizens, associated in people's minds with everything from filth to theft." As the evening wore on and the guests grew exuberant from the wine and the music, the Gypsies started circulating, with practiced eyes choosing the tables with the merriest patrons, those who would tip the most to have their favorite song played. They discreetly pocketed the money, unlike musicians at fairs who like to display it, stuck to their foreheads with spittle or tucked into their hat-bands.

In a village tavern near Szeged we listened to another Gypsy band, much more friendly than those in Budapest. During the intervals, they called us over to their table, offered us food and drink, very pleased by our interest and that Zamur was taking photographs. They asked us about Gypsies in Germany, where they were planning to go some day, if the authorities gave them a visa. If not, they would try to escape: there were people who could get them across the border for 500 dollars. We enquired how much they earned. "Not much," they answered. "Peasants don't like to part with their money, but when they get tipsy themselves, they insist on buying us drinks." "It sometimes happens," the violinist told us, "that I have to down as much as a liter of spirits in an evening if I don't want to get a beating for refusing drinks. When I play until dawn, I'm good for nothing next day. Sometimes I'm so tired from playing and so fuddled from drink I can't even get home: I fall into a ditch at the side of the road and sleep it off." However, he has taught his three sons to play the violin, just as he was taught by his father before him.

Soviet Union

Estimated number: 250,000
Date of arrival: c. 1500
Main centers: Moldavia, Russian Republic
Language: Romany
Religion: Orthodox

Nikolai Erdenko plays the violin in the Gypsy orchestra of the Teater Romen in Moscow. This theater was founded in 1925 when the authorities accepted Gypsies as equal citizens, started printing a newspaper for them, and tried in various ways to help them preserve their identity. In the Stalinist era, however, the system demanded the assimilation of Gypsies, who were expected not to differ in any way from other Soviet citizens. The nomadic way of life was abolished and the Gypsies were settled on various collective farms throughout the Soviet Union. Nikolai told us that there were hardly any Gypsy villages left, except for a few in Moldavia, which became part of the Soviet Union after World War II. Today large Gypsy settlements, such as the one at Kishinev, near Chernobyl, are rare.

"In the Soviet Union, we Gypsy intellectuals – there are quite a few of us who have gained an education – are eagerly following the worldwide movement for the emancipation of Gypsies, their freedom of language and culture. We are only sorry we cannot join in this movement in which Rajko, for example, can take part freely," we were told by Sasha Zavodny, a clerk in a social insurance office in Moscow. In his home the Romany language, spoken by Russian Gypsies, is still used, although not in front of non-Gypsy visitors. We asked whether he thought Russian Gypsies would lose their sense of national identity in the foreseeable future. "No system," he answered, "not even the Soviet, will manage to denationalize the Gypsies, though the authorities are doing their best. We have managed, over the centuries, to preserve our identity in worse conditions. In fact, the Gypsies' national awareness is becoming steadily stronger in the Soviet Union as in other countries. Here we are something like the Jews," Sasha said, "except that, unlike them, we have nowhere to go to, and even if we had, and were allowed to leave, nobody would be delighted to have us. Prejudices against Gypsies are still very strong in this country as well: many regard us a lower race, layabouts, thieves and beggars."

Nikolai Volsaninov, a singer in the Teatar Romen, considers that Russian Gypsies live well: "They complete their schooling and have stopped leading a nomadic life, forbidden by the law of 1953. The old, traditional occupations and crafts have disappeared because of the new way of life. The only thing that has been preserved is Gypsy music, which has always been appreciated in Russia. Gypsy music has stayed, and there is no place of any size without a Gypsy orchestra or band. The older Gypsies regret the changing of the old ways, but the young ones are quite happy as they are. Those who prefer the old way of life can always work as a blacksmith on a collective farm or as an acrobat or something similar. I know for a fact that among the acrobats, animal tamers and keepers in Soviet circuses, there are quite a number of Gypsies. Why should they work outside the state-run organizations when these provide them with a regular job and organized life? Apart from which, Soviet society requires all its citizens to have a permanent place of residence and a steady job, so why should they be exceptions?"

We talked to several other Gypsies about their origins, and found out that they like watching Indian films as they feel an affinity for the way of life and traditions, but as India is a country with many problems, economic and national, they feel no particular bond with it. However, they listened to Rajko's stories of our travels through India with rapt attention, and asked many questions about Gypsies in other countries, firmly convinced that those in the Soviet Union enjoyed a far better life than any others. When we attempted to explain that this was not our impression, mentioning countries such as West Germany, where Gypsies had more rights and on the whole lived much better, they dismissed this as "bourgeois propaganda" directed against the Soviet Union. "Why don't you take your passports," Rajko said, "and go see for yourselves?" Somewhat abashed, the Gypsies admitted that they would certainly do so if the authorities granted them permission to leave the country . . .

"This inability to travel is particularly tough on them," Rajko said. "Imagine Gypsies, wanderers by nature, who can not travel abroad, or even across Russia. Tie a Gypsy down to one place, and you have sentenced him to life imprisonment – a life without movement is no life at all."

Sergei Pavlovich, a worker in the Kishinev waterworks, was of a different opinion: "The notion of roaming and the wish for a miserable Gypsy life is simply an invention of novelists. Gypsies do not want to travel more than any other Soviet citizen. We have an important role in Soviet society because we are good workers, and many are also members of the Party." However, from some Gypsies in Moscow we heard a joke that is told, with slight variations, throughout eastern Europe, about a Gypsy who was invited to become a Party member. In a festively decorated hall, with flags and portraits of Marx, Engels and Lenin, the Party secretary addressed the Gypsy: "You see, although a Gypsy, in our great and democratic society you, too, can become a Party member, and become one of the famous names of our revolution who gave up their lives for the Party and a better future. But you must abandon your bad Gypsy habits if you wish to have this glorious opportunity. Firstly, you must get a steady job." "Oh, all right, I'll work if I have to," the Gypsy answered. "You must stop being a vagabond and beggar." "Very well, I agree," came the answer. "You must never lie or steal." Again he assented. "You must not drink or chase women." When the Gypsy saw that there was no end to the sacrifices, he said: "Stop, don't tell me any more! Let me give up my life for the Party straight away, and to hell with the better future!"

Italy

Estimated number: 85,000
First recorded mention: 1420
Main centers: Northern Italy, Rome (Rom), scattered (Sinti)
Languages: Sinti, Romany
Religions: Catholic, Orthodox, Moslem
Tribal groups: Sinti, Rom

When Gypsies first arrived in Italy in 1422, they were soon banished by the Catholic Church, which did not want to allow this heathen people to settle among the faithful, telling fortunes, practicing magic, believing in vampires... A few decades later, however, they returned and remained in the country, despite cruel persecution. Today, more than 500 years later, the clergy is still interested in Gypsies, but in a different way: the Catholic Church is trying to help them integrate into society, and protect them from discrimination.

In Rome we went to see Rajko's friend, Father Bruno Nicolini, who for the past 30 years has worked with Gypsies, or "nomads" as the Church refers to them. "There are some 85,000 of them in Italy, divided into two groups — the Sinti, who have lived here for centuries, and the Roma, mostly from Yugoslavia," he told us. "The former are in a better position; the latter have brought many problems, like the scandal about the sale of children. Maybe you know about it: some Yugoslav Roma bought children from their compatriots and used them for thieving. This has made our work much more difficult, because the authorities are now reluctant to set aside camping places for them and do anything to improve their position."

In Pescara, south of Rome, we went to visit a Sinti settlement, and called on Father Lizza, who put us up in a seminary. In the evening, sitting around the refectory table with ten or so other priests, we had a long and interesting discussion about the life of Gypsies and our book. First thing in the morning, Father Lizza took us to meet them. On the way he told us that he had been working among them for many years and knew most of them by name. "They live in small houses on the outskirts of the town, because they want to have yards in which to keep their dogs and horses. In the past the horses served as draft animals because the Gypsies worked as carriers, but now they are used for racing or to pull tourists around town in open carriages." Father Lizza entered the settlement first to explain why we were there. "Otherwise they might not be very friendly to anyone carrying cameras. Taking photographs is usually connected with newspapers, and these rarely have a good word for

Every year on May 24–26 Gypsies from all over the world make a pilgrimage to the south of France to the village of Saintes Maries de la Mer, on the Ile de la Camargue in the river Rhône. Some 20,000 people, about 10,000 of them Gypsies, come to pay their respects to the two Marys of Bethany and to St Sarah, patron saint of the Gypsies. There are some 300,000 Gypsies in France today, about 40% of them nomadic. The first are recorded as arriving in Paris in 1427.

no longer where I left them: they have been chased away. Then I spend the whole day looking for them. I once searched for three whole days because we'd forgotten to arrange a meeting place in case they were moved on...'' When we asked him about his life, he said: "I'd like to settle somewhere and send the kids to school. They don't learn anything like this. We can't travel any longer: there's no field where you can camp in peace. There used to be a lot of free, uncultivated land, but today everywhere is overpopulated.'' We asked Gilbert if they had been to any other country – maybe it was easier and better somewhere else. Yes, he told us, they had been to Spain, Italy, and even England, but it was the same everywhere. "There's no place for us on this earth,'' he commented. "It's time for the Gypsy race to disappear.'' When we asked how they earned their living, Gilbert refused to talk to us any further, but a young man standing nearby answered instead: "We work a little, steal a little, tell fortunes or beg, depending on our need.'' As we talked, a patrol car appeared, and we decided it was time for us, too, to move on.

As we approached Saintes Maries de la Mer, the gloomy picture of Gypsy life was suddenly transformed. It may have had a lot to do with the brilliantly sunny weather, the general carefree atmosphere and the excitement of the Gypsies and other visitors to the festival. They had come from all parts of France and Europe in order to forget their troubles for a few days, have fun, meet members of their scattered families. Some 10,000 Gypsies gathered in this little place which, out of season, has only 5,000 or so inhabitants. Two days in advance they were already occupying all the available parking space and the seats in bars and cafés, where they were drinking, singing and boisterously hailing one another. "When all this is over,'' Rajko said, "they'll set off in various directions, though some won't return where they came from. Somewhere along the way, on an impulse, they'll decide to try another place, or even country. Having no property or home, they've nothing to lose, and if they left any members of the family behind, they'll send for them.''

The day of the saint's feast dawned, and the Gypsies already gathered were joined by 10,000 tourists, so that Zamur had his work cut out to take photographs without interference.

Spain

Estimated number: 800,000
First recorded mention: 1425
Main centers: Madrid, Barcelona, Granada, etc.
Language: Kalo
Religion: Catholic
Tribal group: Kale

In Barcelona, our Gypsy connection, Ines, first took us to the Quento Tkalaya settlement inhabited by about 700 Gypsies. "The municipal authorities designated this place as their temporary abode,'' she told us, "in order to stop them roaming all over town and raising their shacks wherever they want to.'' Our arrival was immediately noticed and several men moved menacingly towards us. Ines's explanation that we were writing a book on the Gypsies' difficult life and position did not help: they obviously connected the arrival of camera-toting strangers with the police, and that boded no good. Since Spanish Gypsies speak Kalo, a mixture of Romany, Spanish and words from other languages and dialects, Rajko was unable to intercede with his brethren. We were forced to split up, Zamur circling the settlement with his cameras to enter it alone at some other point, and the rest of us going to see Hortensia Fernandez, an acquaintance of our guide. The young woman, a child in her arms, let us into her tiny home, furnished only with two chairs, a table and a bed: her stove and pots and pans were in the yard behind the house. We found out that she worked as a washerwoman and cleaner in other

161   This celebration is connected with an event purported to have taken place in AD 42, when St Mary Jacobe and St Mary Salome, the mothers of the Apostles John and James, are said to have landed on this part of the Mediterranean coast, having drifted from the Holy Land in a tiny boat without oars or sail. With them in the boat was a swarthy "Egyptian" servant girl, Sarah. The Gypsies incorporated vestiges of the Indian Durga cult into the Catholic feast, hence the joint celebration.

162   The Gypsies ride their horses into the sea forming a semi-circle and symbolically protecting the images of the saints being brought from the waves. On the first day of the feast they protect the Marys, the biblical "sisters" of the Virgin, on the second, the dark-skinned Sarah. By tradition they submerge the saints three times. This pilgrimage, the oldest in France, was joined by the Gypsies in the 19th century. The cult of Sarah is purely Gypsy folklore since, unlike her two fellow-voyagers, she is not recognized by the Church as a saint.

163   Black Sarah is prepared for the ritual, being carefully dressed by chosen Gypsies, who will carry her out of the crypt and later from the sea. Thus clothed and crowned, the dark-skinned "saint" will be the subject of adoration for two whole days. The Gypsies all attempt to touch or kiss her clothing or face, since this is believed to bring good health.

164 Followed by large numbers of Gypsies, and lately also of tourists, the saints are borne by Gypsies on their shoulders, behind the Holy Cross (on the first day the two Marys, on the second and third, Sarah). This cult originated in India, where the Black Virgin is called Durga or Kali. Vestiges of it can be found in other European countries – in Spain and in Yugoslavia, where the effigy is called Bibiaca, which in Romany means ''aunt'' or ''lady''.

165 St
her shri
crypt of
the two
itself. W
Sara-la-
chanting
Gypsies
help us
all the n
not only
the cou
to see t

166, 16
Mer hou
which l
process
whole
and tha
in the v
attentic
of cand
heat, s
fervor
effigy.

175   The members of an extended family, scattered all over Europe, met here to discuss various problems, from feuds, jobs and moves to other countries to the wedding of the youngest daughter.

176　A large number of flashy Gypsy cars with the most diverse licence plates and caravans of all shapes and sizes, from the oldest and cheapest to the most elaborate and luxuriously equipped, mirror differences in the living standard of Gypsies in the areas from which they come. Parked along the coast up to the church itself, they made up the largest mobile Gypsy camp to be seen anywhere in Europe.

177, 178　Gypsies from all over Europe were there, dressed in the clothes and speaking the language of the country they live in, but when discussing matters with other groups, they communicated mostly in Romany. We saw men and women of all ages and nationalities gathered together: circus millionaires, artisans of all kinds, musicians, lawyers and poets – a microcosm of the whole Gypsy world.

178

179 The celebration of St. Sarah is an occasion to show off one's Sunday best, to meet scattered family and friends, to see and be seen . . .

180 Innocencio Amaya Jimenez lives in the San Martin barrio on the outskirts of Barcelona. He was born here 64 years ago, and in common with most of the other 25,000 Gypsies in Barcelona, makes his living by collecting rags, paper, scrap-iron and other waste recycled for use by the local industry. An estimated 800,000 Gypsies, or as the Spaniards call them, Gitanos, live in Spain today. The first tribes are thought to have come to the Iberian peninsula in the early 15th century.

182

181 We photographed this group of Gypsies belonging to Innocencio's numerous extended family in front of the house in which they found a temporary home. In this house, vacated and marked for demolition, they will spend the winter until one day the bulldozers force them to search for another, similar abode. "No matter how short a time we stay here," they told us, "it pays — we have a roof over our heads and it doesn't cost us anything. There's no water or electricity anyway."

182 In his younger days, before he got asthma, Innocencio Amaya Jimenez used to be an excellent dancer of Flamenco, a Gypsy dance of Spanish origin to which the Gitanos brought their restlessness and melancholy, their wild fiery temperament. The authentic version is performed without any instrumental accompaniment or castanettes, only with the clapping of hands and piercing, throaty singing. It was not until the 19th century that this dance began to be accompanied by the guitar.

183 An essential ingredient of the Flamenco is the rhythmic rapping of the dancer's steps, performed at incredible speed. This Gypsy, impelled by a sudden urge, tore the door off a house so that his steps would be heard to better effect. When the Flamenco starts with its clapping and singing, the Gypsies of Spain, all their troubles forgotten, are transported into the realms of caravans, horses and voyages, and by hopes of a better tomorrow.

184

184 To compare it with what we had seen in the Gypsy camp, we visited the famous El Cordobes Club, named after the celebrated Gypsy bull-fighter, a night spot popular with American tourists. Sumptuously attired, under the glow of the spotlights the performers held the audience spellbound with their passionate dancing, their steps echoing like gunshots through the club.

185

185　In the dressing-room, Dolores de la Santa told us that she was conscious of being among those few fortunate ones who manage to rise from the Gypsy camps to the spotlights of Flamenco shows all over Spain.

186　On the outskirts of Barcelona we visited the Quento Tkalaya camp, which numbers about 700 Gypsies. The city authorities installed electricity and running water, while the Gypsies provide their own roofs over their heads. Since Franco's death, the government has made an effort to improve their living conditions by building settlements for them which look less and less like their traditional ghettos. In this settlement we met girls who earn their living by dancing the Flamenco on the squares and in the taverns of Barcelona, and young men who try their luck as bull-fighters, a very lucrative profession. Almost half of all the torreadors in Spain are Gypsies. "The thrill of excitement draws them to this profession. They are excellent at it, fearless because they have nothing to lose," we were told by Father Antonio Garcia Ortez, whom we met in the settlement.

187   Hortensia Fernandez does the cleaning, washing and ironing in well-off families, thus helping to support herself, her two children and husband. Antonio works in a junkyard, removing undamaged parts from cars and selling them to individuals and mechanics as spares. The couple are saving up for tickets to Bogota, where they have relatives. During our travels in Spain we met several Gypsies who were planning to emigrate to South America, where the way of life suits them and they encounter fewer prejudices. The Spaniards were, in fact, the first to resettle Gypsies overseas – the earliest record of them in South America dates from 1581.

188   Pedro Hernandez breeds pigeons, keeping about 60 of them in his dovecote which is, in fact, part of his house. Every Saturday he goes to the market to sell them, together with other pigeon-fanciers. Tumbler pigeons are particularly sought after, being both beautiful birds and amusing acrobats. It

is difficult for Gypsies to keep pigeons, for the same reason they keep their hens cooped up. ''When one of my birds lands on someone's roof, it usually ends up on the dinner table,'' says Pedro. ''They ate my champion tumbler like that. I suppose in the end I'll give up pigeons and try my hand at something else.''

250

193, 194   In a suburb of Madrid we witnessed a family quarrel: on returning from town, the Gypsy found the women chatting instead of going from house to house telling fortunes. He was about to teach them a lesson when the police arrived, putting an end to the family strife: they immediately closed ranks against their age-old enemy – authority. Residents of the suburb had called the police to chase the Gypsies away from their area. The Gypsies complained, swore, argued, offered money, but finally had to give in and leave.

195   In the suburbs of Barcelona the municipal authorities have constructed many new blocks of flats to house the homeless, including Gypsies. The latter immediately put up fences on their apartment balconies, to stop neighbors entering uninvited. In their traditional settlements all doors are kept open, for Gypsies rarely steal from one another. In the city, it seems, this law has changed.

251

people's houses, while her husband was employed in a junkyard. They hoped to be able to emigrate in a few months to Bogota, where they had relatives and life was said to be easier.

Under the Socialist government, the Gypsies' position had somewhat improved, as they were included in the party's program, Ines explained, but the initial results had not been particularly encouraging, since the criteria applied were inappropriate to Gypsies. Efforts to provide them with a roof over their heads, for example, had been misguided: their settlements in Barcelona were razed to the ground and the Gypsies moved to highrise blocks on the outskirts. Unused to this kind of life, they vandalized the buildings, breaking down the walls between their apartments and those of relatives, placing bars on windows and balconies adjoining other neighbors . . . Soon the buildings looked more like prisons. It would have been better, Rajko felt, to build even settlements like Quento Tkalaya and provide them with running water and electricity, a medical center, a school, and so on. Gypsies do not see a solution to their difficulties in being scattered all over the country and thus wiped out as a nation. This, Rajko told us, was the policy of almost all west European countries: to drown the Gypsies in a sea of other people. Even if Gypsies in this way acquired the same rights and opportunities as the other citizens of these countries, they could not be happy, plucked out by their roots, losing their identity and their world. Instead, we should be helping to eliminate the blighting effects of the misery and squalor in which they have always lived.

Over the next few days we visited several other settlements. One Sunday afternoon in the San Martin barrio of Barcelona, we came across a group of Gypsies dancing the Flamenco to music blaring from a radio inside one of the houses. Innocencio Amaya Jimenes, dressed in his best white suit, performed the steps slowly while the many members of his family clapped their hands to the rhythm. Seeing us, they stopped for a moment and then, unlike the Gypsies we had last seen, clamored to have their photographs taken. Ines explained that this was because they were all wearing their Sunday best and felt they looked presentable. While Zamur took pictures, Ines, Rajko and I talked to the Gypsies. Attracted by the noise and excitement, a drunken Gypsy came over to us. He shook his head, dissatisfied with Innocencio's rendering of the fiery Flamenco. Occasionally he stepped forward, clapping his hands and stamping his feet, then retired again, displeased. When the music reached its climax, our inebriated friend dashed over and ripped the front door off its hinges, threw it down and started dancing, satisfied that the rapping of his heels could now be heard clearly. Much to our surprise Innocencio, whose front door was being stamped on in the dust, did not seem at all put out. After two hours, there was not much left of the door. Exhausted by the dancing, the drunken Gypsy made off unsteadily for home, stopping to tap his feet every few yards, then tottering on, until he disappeared from view.

The following evening we went to the famous El Cordobes night club where several Gypsies perform Flamenco for American tourists . . . Dolores de la Santa agreed to talk to us, as she got ready for her performance. She had been born and raised in a settlement similar to Quento Tkalaya, and her family still lived in poverty as her salary was not high enough to improve their position very much. Still, she considered herself extremely fortunate to work in a well-known night club.

The Flamenco (from *felehmengu*, "village singer" in Arabic) evolved in Andalusia in the 18th century as an expression of the Gypsies' feelings and way of life. Its essence is the *cante hondo* or "profound song", a synthesis of east and west, but probably originating in India. The *cante hondo*, epitomiz-

196   Ten-year-old Manuela, remininscent here of a painting by Murillo, works "in partnership" with her elder brother, Domingo. In the evening, she makes the rounds of Barcelona cafés selling posies, while he supplies the flowers, waits outside to collect the takings, and serves as her protector.

ing the pain and sorrow, the physical and spiritual suffering of the Gitanos, became known to a wider public only after Charles III's ordinance abolishing laws on the persecution of Gypsies in 1783. Until then, it was sung within the Gitanos' communities, as a ritual and cult song. In time the Flamenco was adapted for public entertainment, and is now a major tourist attraction.

On the Plaza Real square in Barcelona dark-skinned youths, after glancing furtively about them, offered passers-by hashish for 500 pesetas. We watched them stop the occasional young man, talk, exchange little packets for money and disappear. According to Ines, they worked for the "mafia": when caught by the police, they were unable to supply names or information as they only ever contacted one person. Once in prison, they were simply written off – there were many unemployed young Gypsies ready to sell dope in order to earn a few pesetas.

The situation is similar in other towns: Madrid, Bilbao, Burgos, Granada... In the settlement of Vicalcaro in Madrid alone, there are around 70,000 Gypsies. Perhaps a third of Spanish Gypsies still lead a nomadic way of life, but their dilapidated caravans (trailers), usually factory-made, are drawn by automobiles. In a suburb of Madrid we came upon a parked caravan and three Gypsy women in long skirts sitting on the pavement, chatting, in front of some new apartment blocks. Several of the residents, Spaniards, came over and told them to leave immediately – obviously afraid they would camp in the neighborhood. The women protested that they were only waiting for their husbands to return from town and would then be off. When we showed an interest in the argument, the residents told us they had to chase the Gypsies away at once or others would follow. "They should all be deported," one declared. "You can never be certain they won't steal something or do some damage." When we asked him where the Gypsies should be banished to, he answered "where they came from," but admitted he didn't know where that was. We asked the Gypsy women the same question. "We've always been in Spain," they insisted. When told that all Gypsies had originally come from India, they were offended – maybe others had, but they themselves had always lived in Spain. We asked what their husbands were doing in town. It appeared they were selling second-hand things they found or bought cheaply along the way. Were had they come from, and where were they going? We would have to ask their husbands that, they replied. They told us they were fortune-tellers, and offered to read our palms if we had the time and inclination, and were ready to pay for this service. We all agreed. "You are from a distant land. Your children ask their mother about you. Where is our father? There is an enemy who wants to destroy your marriage, and tells terrible lies about you to your wife. But she doesn't believe him. She believes only you. And here is fortune smiling at you – fortune like money, or maybe something else..." Later we discovered we had all three heard more or less the same story. We gave them some money, but they seemed dissatisfied with the amount. Rajko told us it was an unwritten rule – Gypsies never say "enough", and always ask for more than has been given.

As we were saying goodbye, a Gypsy appeared and started shouting at the women. We gathered that he was scolding them for chatting idly instead of telling fortunes in the neighboring buildings. At this point a police car arrived, probably called by the residents, and the police ordered the Gypsies to follow them immediately. In the argument that ensued, one of the women even offered them money. When their protests and pleas proved unavailing, they got into the caravan and drove off behind the police car. "What about the two Gypsies still in town?" we asked Rajko. "Don't worry," he laughed, "they'll meet elsewhere, as previously arranged. Gypsies foresee such eventualities and use secret signs as messages." This was later confirmed by another group of Spanish Gypsies we met on the road. They told us that secret signs and markings were left on each site, different signs for each group. Two stones and a twig meant that they had been chased away by the police and would be back as soon as possible. The message could be translated as: wait for us here.

"This secret language was invented mainly to foil the authorities, the Gypsies' greatest enemies," Rajko told us. "Because Gypsies live outside the organized state, in order to survive they have to outwit the law, and this they can do only if they can communicate and make plans without the authorities knowing."

Austria

Estimated number: 40,000
First recorded mention: 1376
Main centers: Vienna, Burgenland
Languages: Sinti, Romany
Religions: Catholic, Orthodox
Tribal groups: Sinti, Rom (Kalderash, Lovar)

In Vienna we were warmly welcomed by Rajko's sister, Zorica, one of the 20,000 Yugoslav Gypsies who moved to this neighboring country over the past 20 years, especially in the period when Austria had a labor shortage. She went to Vienna in 1966 and got a job on the Austrian railways, having graduated from a secondary commercial school in Yugoslavia. In this respect, she is rather an exception: most Gypsies there are unqualified, and often illiterate as well. In Vienna, Zorica met Gerhard Bonner, an Austrian, and married him. When we went to visit them, she and Rajko spoke in Romany and Serbo-Croatian, while her four-year-old son interrupted in German. Gerhard chatted with Rajko about Belgrade, and the politics and economy of the country he visits every year with his wife and son. They spoke in German as he has not learned Romany, although he says he intends to. We asked Gerhard what opinion he had had of Gypsies before his marriage: "Before I met Zorica, I knew nothing of Gypsies, and never thought much about them. I used to see Yugoslav Roma and Austrian Sinti and had the same attitude to them as other Austrians." The Yugoslav Gypsies, being mostly illiterate, are given the worst jobs: sweeping streets, cleaning out sewers... Most live in mobile homes, shacks, huts and tents, though others are starting to free themselves economically and educationally from their heritage. The Sinti, who arrived in Austria several centuries ago, naturally differ from the Roma in religion and language. Being generally more prosperous, they look down on these Yugoslav newcomers and avoid mixing with them.

According to Zorica, both the Sinti and the Roma live relatively well in Austria, and some of them, particularly second-hand furniture and antique dealers and restaurant musicians, are quite successful. She took us to several places where Gypsies gather, such as Mexico-Platz, where they sell second-hand goods, some bought cheaply, some smuggled or even "borrowed". In the Prater, where Gypsies are park maintenance workers, lead ponies or call children to the swings, we met a young man from Sarajevo named Alija. He told us that a "court hearing" was to be held in the Prater the next Sunday. "Our problems are our own. Why should foreigners judge us?" he said. Apparently, one Gypsy had seduced his neighbor's wife. The court would decide whether he should return her to her husband or pay the man compensation for the shame. On the Sunday we arrived at the appointed place and time, but waited in vain. We wondered whether we had made a mistake, but Zorica explained that Gypsies had a different sense of time. "If they tell you they will meet to discuss matters in the morning, it can be five in the afternoon before they all get together."

Austrian Gypsies, the Sinti, rarely admit to their race, probably because of their experiences in World War II. Numbering from five to six thousand, they mostly live about 60 miles north of Vienna. Except in coloring, they differ little from other Austrians. The majority are factory workers, but some have typical Gypsy occupations: collecting paper and scrap-iron, selling second-hand goods at markets, etc.

"Before I left for Austria," Zorica recalled, "Grandma Javorka told my fortune from the coffee grounds: I would meet a blond man who would not be of Gypsy blood, but I'd come to love him and he would be my man, my husband. At that time there had never been a case in our family of anyone marrying a Gadja, a non-Gypsy, so I was very surprised she should predict such a thing. I still can't decide whether it was really some sixth sense, whether Grandma, an illiterate old woman, foresaw the great changes that have taken place in the lives of Gypsies and in their relations with the citizens of their host country..."

West Germany

Estimated number: 80,000
First recorded mention: 1417
Main centers: West Berlin, Heidelberg, Frankfurt, Munich
Languages: Romany, Sinti
Religions: Catholic, Protestant, Orthodox, Moslem
Tribal groups: Sinti, Rom

In the years when West Germany was in pressing need of unskilled laborers, hundreds of shacks sprang up almost overnight on the outskirts of Darmstadt. Built of planks, corrugated iron, sheets of plastic and other rejects of the affluent consumer society, they were occupied by Gypsies from Yugoslavia, Poland, Hungary, Czechoslovakia... The authorities in Darmstadt and other cities were confronted with the problem of how to check the proliferation of such slums, and what to do with the 30,000 or so Gypsies who had come to the country in hope of a better life. Hans Neubauer of Düsseldorf, one of the 50,000 German Sinti, told us that in this particular case, the German police had tried to evict the Roma on several occasions, but had failed.

Hans took us to a neat new settlement of some 40 homes in a cul-de-sac on the outskirts of Düsseldorf, built to house German Sinti employed in the local industry. Having been in Germany for several centuries, most of the Sinti have gradually become integrated in the life of the country and are regarded with more benevolence than the newcomers, the Roma, who brought with them all their Gypsy characteristics and customs, some charming and interesting, but most simply distasteful to their hosts. The German Gypsies, the Sinti, dislike and do not mix with the Roma because of their different lifestyles, economic and language differences. The Sinti speak a Romany dialect with a large admixture of German, while the Romany language of the newcomers contains many words borrowed from countries in which they stopped on their long journey from India.

We spent a morning visiting in this housing development and talking to the Gypsy women who regularly gather in one another's houses to drink coffee. Each garden had a caravan (trailer) in it. As one of the women explained: "We still like to travel, but now we can do so only in the summer because our men work." The caravans were decorated with pictures of prancing horses, the Gypsy symbol of freedom and movement. Their husbands, we learned, were employed either in factories or in fun-fairs, still very popular in Germany. "Some work in circuses," dark-skinned Helga told us, "like my brothers and our parents before them."

Thomas Wenzel, who has a little furrier's shop in Ulm, spoke eloquently about the position of his fellow Sinti: "The general democratic trend in Germany has affected the life of the Sinti. You should not mix them up with the Roma, who are "guest workers" and, as such, meet with different, problems. You could say that we, the Sinti in Germany, are the richest, on

"Gypsy Girl", oil painting by Boccaccio Boccaccino, early 16th century, in the Uffizi Gallery, Florence.

256

average, in the world. Because of what we suffered during the war, when 70,000 Sinti and about half a million Gypsies from other countries were wiped out, the Sinti are now freed from paying taxes on any kind of business they run. This is how the Germans are compensating for their treatment of Gypsies in the war. But in a way, the economic security discourages Sinti from working hard, and especially from getting a good education for their children. It also lessens their interest in the Gypsy question and organization, in the further emancipation of Gypsies outside of Germany and in it. They rarely use the Sinti language, and the younger ones hardly know it."

Johann Maier, a traveling Gypsy, spoke of the everyday problems encountered on the road: "It often happens that one of us stops his caravan in a public parking place, because the children are hungry and crying, and the women want to cook them something to eat. Then along comes our friend in the green uniform and chases us away. But he doesn't say where we should go: we're not allowed to enter official camping sites. Most judges punish Sinti more severely than non-Gypsies. In the schools our children are despised, sworn at and often beaten up. And prejudice stops Sinti getting the opportunity to learn the trade of their choice. We want no special privileges: we just want the right to be accepted by society with our own culture, traditions and language." His wife added timidly: "I even saw a sign in Mannheim that said 'Keep the surrounding area clean. Deposit rubbish and ash inside the containers. Do not behave like Gypsies!'"

Seventy-year-old Oscar Rose lives near Heidelberg. During the war he was sent to the Bergen Belsen camp, which was founded, he says, before the camps for Jews. His numerous family were among the half a million Gypsies who died in such camps, and he himself only survived by a miracle. He spoke very highly of Willi Brandt who, after the war, met with Sinti representatives several times and strove for reparations for the Gypsies who, unlike the Jews and other peoples, have never received any. Willi Brandt demanded the same rights for the Gypsies and did much to bring their problems to the attention of the German government...

Romani Rose, who is 39, is the president of the German Sinti and Roma Organization, which campaigns for equal rights and tries to check discrimination against the Roma, either by Sinti or by Germans. "In the case of the Sinti, it is only the discrimination of the Germans that has to be fought," he told us. How was it, we asked, that German Sinti showed open hostility towards their brethren from East European and Balkan countries? "This is part of the Gypsy misfortune," he answered. "The behaviour of some Gypsies towards others can be worse than that of non-Gypsies towards our race as a whole... The Sinti are much better off than the Roma, who have only recently arrived, and so regard them with contempt. The Roma often live in tents and slums, some are thieves or beggars, and the Sinti shun them, not wanting to be identified with these brethren for whom they have no feeling because they have had no contacts. To the Germans, however, both are simply *Zigeuner*, the only difference being that some speak German and others do not."

Rajko, who spent several months in West Germany studying the Gypsies' living conditions, commented that everything was relative: compared to the life they lead in other countries, even the Roma are better off in Germany than anywhere else. The movement of the Greens in Germany pays particular attention to the position of the Gypsies, demanding equal rights for them and the abolition of the practice by the German police of keeping special files on them, considering this to be a continuation of racism and the treatment of Gypsies as an "asocial people".

The Protestant, especially Evangelical, Churches actively help the Roma and Sinti even though very few are of this faith. Several years ago the

Evangelical Church of Hessen and Nassau organized a Gypsy Music Festival in Darmstadt, with the idea of giving Gypsies a chance to meet and exchange news and opinions, but also of educating and informing the non-Gypsy population about this different culture and way of life. The aim was to provide an opportunity for both sides to get together, discuss problems and try to solve them; in the course of which many prejudices would be overcome. Somewhat to the surprise of the Sinti, the festival was very well attended by non-Gypsies, who took part in the forum and discussions. This led to some improvements: better relations between individuals and promises from politicians to allow the Sinti to travel and camp without discrimination. The town of Darmstadt agreed to provide both a transit and a permanent camping site for the Sinti.

"The festival lasted four wonderful days, with many famous Gypsy musicians taking part, an exhibition of photographs and documents relating to Gypsies, an open forum about the social, political and cultural problems of Gypsies, showings of films, videos and television programs dealing with them, a children's afternoon when non-Gypsy and Gypsy children played together, and even a flea-market," Anita Schmidt from Frankfurt told us. "The idea was to inform the German public of the true situation: that discrimination against Gypsies didn't end with World War II, that authorities and individuals were making life very difficult for travelers, that many are faced with the collapse of their traditional occupations because of the changing economic and industrial situation, and that it is difficult for them to get training for other jobs. Some changes have been made but we are still waiting for the important ones."

Netherlands

From Germany we set off to see how Gypsies live in the Netherlands. Rajko already knew a good deal about this: at international gatherings he had talked at length with several Dutch priests who worked with the so-called travelers. From them he learned that there were some 35,000 Gypsies in the Netherlands, the majority Sinti and Manush, but also some Roma – Kalderash or Lovar – relative newcomers from the Soviet Union, Hungary, Romania and Yugoslavia.

We made our way to Breda, to one of the 20 or so Gypsy camps in the Netherlands. It was on the outskirts of the town, well arranged and tidy, with about 30 mobile homes. At the suggestion of some townspeople, we asked for a man named Weiss, and soon found him in a neat, specklessly clean caravan with brand-new furniture. When told the purpose of our visit, he was highly offended, and shouted that he wanted no connection with Gypsies. We soon managed to clear up the misunderstanding: it turned out that he objected to being identified with the Kalderash and Lovar, who do not have a particularly savory reputation in the Netherlands. The Sinti had arrived centuries before and fitted into Dutch society, whereas the newcomers "only made trouble". "Your Yugoslav Gypsies are thieves, layabouts and filthy, and give all Gypsies a bad name," Weiss told us. "They should all be deported; they're not for life in the Netherlands." After this our conversation followed a smoother course until we asked whether he knew that all Gypsies had originally come from India, even the Sinti to which he belonged. Dutch Gypsies, he angrily remonstrated, had nothing to do with India, and when we asked him to tell us where they came from, he answered: "The Gypsies are a special kind of good people who are from the countries they live in. They

Estimated number: 35,000
First recorded mention: 1420
Language: Romany
Religions: Protestant, Orthodox
Tribal groups: Sinti, Rom (Lovar, Kalderash)

differ from others only in being unselfish, giving without taking. They do their best to amuse and entertain others.

"They are musical and play the violin, and whoever plays music is a good person." When I asked how it happened that both he and his eight children had darker complexions than the Dutch, Weiss had a ready answer: "You three differ in color as well: he (Zamur) is fair, you are brown-haired, and he (Rajko) is dark like me." When we observed that this was natural since Rajko was a Gypsy, he changed the subject. We soon met his numerous family, some of them grown up and living in separate caravans. His son, Jan, a pleasant and helpful young man, was less dogmatic and did not mind the connection with Indian Gypsies, Roma or any others. On the contrary, he asked many questions and showed an interest in their position, number and way of life. He had taken over his father's business, collecting wrecked cars and selling the parts as spares. He had the Gypsy love of horses and showed us the colt he was raising, with which he spent all his spare time. It was touching to see the two of them in the yard full of rusted scrap and car parts. Jan introduced us to his sister, Luana, married to a non-Gypsy from the same camp, one of the so-called travelers, of whom there are quite a few in the Netherlands. In the scrupulously clean and tidy large caravan, resembling a typical Dutch home, this beautiful young woman sat down barefooted at the piano and played us a few tunes.

Jan told us that the Church took care of camps such as this one. Together with the municipal authorities and social workers, it helps to get camps set up and maintained, sees that children attend school regularly, extends legal and other aid if anyone gets into trouble with the law, and provides the old and sick with adequate medical·and other care. "Much has been done for Gypsies in the Netherlands," Jan told us. "But I agree with Father that the newcomers are responsible for our unpopularity. I sometimes meet them, but can't talk to them – we speak Sinti with a lot of Dutch words, they speak something different."

Hearing of our adventures journeying in various countries, he said that this was a good idea: "Maybe some day I'll take my caravan and travel the world – even to India."

197   This Gypsy girl has brought for sale second-hand goods discarded by housewives or bought cheaply. She travels once a month to Belgrade in neighboring Yugoslavia to collect wares from members of her family, who roam Vojvodina villages in search of old oil lamps and similar articles much in demand in Austria.

198   In the Prater, Vienna's famous park, we met many Gypsies, both Austrian Sinti and Yugoslav and East European Roma. Because of differences in language and way of life the two groups do not mix, though both work as attendants and fair-hands. Other Gypsies come there to relax and enjoy themselves on the swings and merry-go-rounds after a day's work cleaning the streets of Vienna.

199   Despite the existence of automated "hi-tec" amusement parks, the old-fashioned swings and merry-go-rounds, which Gypsies make themselves, are still quite popular. After a day's work at the factory, young Germans and Gypsies come to this fun-fair in Düsseldorf to enjoy themselves and mingle with their peers. In recent years there has been a greater degree of socializing between Germans and Gypsies, and an increasing number of mixed marriages.

United Kingdom and Ireland

Gypsies are believed to have arrived in England around 1490. One band crossed to Ireland while another went north into Scotland. At first, as everywhere on the continent, they were regarded benevolently as pilgrims, and alms were given them, but soon this sentiment changed. As early as 1530, in the reign of Henry VIII, we find the following official report on them: "Diverse and many outlandish people calling themselves Egyptians, using no craft or feat or merchandise... have gone from shire to shire and place to place in great company and used great and subtle means to deceive the people, bearing them in hand that they by palmistry could tell men's and women's fortunes, and many times by craft and subtlety have deceived the people of their money and have also committed many heinous felonies and robberies to the great hurt and deceit of the people they have come among."

An account dated 1528 claims that there were 10,000 Gypsies in the British Isles by that year. Laws against them were passed in 1541, and their persecution continued, albeit less severely, up to the 17th century. As an example, in May 1596, under the provision of the statutes against Egyptians or Bohemians (as the Gypsies were then called in England), a company of 196

Estimated number: 50,000 (U.K.)
                   20,000 (Ireland)
Date of arrival: c. 1490
Main centers: Most large cities
Language: Romany
Religions: Protestant, Catholic

200   Apart from selling second-hand goods
and antiques, working in municipal sanitation
departments and at fun-fairs, Gypsies can
also be found in circuses as animal tamers,
trainers, and acrobats — most often tight-rope
walkers, a profession common among their
kin in India. One of the first groups to reach
Germany, in the 15th century, is recorded as
giving acrobatic performances in
Magdeburg.

201 A fire in the Gypsy settlement in Düsseldorf swallowed up the huts made of boards and other inflammable material. The flames engulfed everything in just a few minutes: the Gypsies could only stand helplessly watching their homes destroyed. Fortunately there were no victims, as there normally are in such fires. Next day they had to look for somewhere else to raise their shacks, and accused the police and municipal authorities of starting the fire, while the latter blamed the Gypsies' own carelessness.

203 Our connection in Germany, Hans Neubauer, took us to a new Gypsy settlement in Düsseldorf. The city authorities had built some 40 houses for German Sinti employed in the local industry. This was the first time on our travels that we found the living conditions of Gypsies on a par with those of other citizens.

202 Luana is married to a non-Gypsy "traveler" who lives in the same camp as her family, a not infrequent situation in the Netherlands. In an expensively decorated mobile home, she entertained us on the piano. She does not go out to work, and in many ways resembles an ordinary Dutch housewife.

205

204   Jan, Luana's brother, has taken over his father's business, dealing in wrecked cars. Beside the car dump he keeps a colt which occupies much of his free time.

205   The first groups of Gypsies arrived in the Low Countries in 1420. More than five centuries later some 35,000 of them live on the territory of the present-day Netherlands. Known as ''travelers'', they mostly live in mobile homes and prefabricated accommodation, often provided by local authorities. Even in these surroundings, the Gypsies retain their desire to keep horses.

206   The vardos or Gypsy caravan is a real work of art. Gypsies invest great amounts of money and much time keeping it spick and span, for the sake of prestige. The vardos is built by special craftsmen from seasoned oak, and decorated with beautifully worked brass and copper articles. They are now rarely made and already represent collectors' prizes. The gay colors and patterns bring to mind the Gypsy carts in India. Gypsies first came to Great Britain in about 1490; today an estimated 50,000 of them live there.

207 Most British Gypsies are still nomadic or semi-sedentary. By the Gypsy Council's own reckoning, about 80% of the travelers are illiterate. Although the Caravan Sites Act makes it obligatory for county councils to provide sites for Gypsies, some 35% of all British Gypsies still have no sites on which they can legally park. Illustrated: scrap-metal merchant Richard Johnson and his family are settling down for the night in Dorset. They will have to move at dawn, before the owner of the property calls in the police.

208 Each June, Appleby, an ancient little town on the river Eden in northwest England, is inundated by thousands of Gypsies and hundreds of farmers, who come for the New Fair to trade horses. Appleby campers occupy an area far in excess of what has officially been allocated for the occasion, bringing protests from the landowners. The Romans encouraged horse fairs and markets in this region as long as 2000 years ago.

209, 210 Before being brought to market, the horses are washed and well groomed. Gypsies sometimes rub a special oil into the coat to make it glossier and some even use old tricks, such as giving the animal alcohol to make it seem livelier, or pouring fine sawdust into the horse's ears to make it twitch its ears and hold its head high.

211   Gypsies arrived in Ireland in 1490, when a large group crossed from England. In 1665, when Gypsies were supposed to be banished from England to the West Indies, many escaped to Ireland, but on several occasions Irish Gypsies crossed into England as well. The largest group did so in the early 1960s, following the Irish government's attempt to settle them. Travelers in Ireland are divided into Gypsies and Tinkers, the latter having come into being as a result of Cromwell's scorched earth policy. Scholars claim that it is difficult to draw an ethnic line between them as they have traveled and mixed together for so long.

212   This Tinker family stopped on the road in County Cork to prepare a meal and settle down for a long foggy night. Next day they will go to Cork to sell their ornamental metal wares. Irish travelers usually deal in scrap-iron, old furniture and horses.

persons was brought before a Justice of the Peace in Yorkshire; 106, being adults, were condemned to death because, as the document set forth, they were idle persons, "some of them the Queen's natural born subjects . . . who lead idle lives wandering about the country in company with these Gypsies, using a speech that is not understood by the other inhabitants of the realm, and obeying laws that are not the laws of the realm". This may account for the quantity of English blood now flowing in the veins of some 50,000 Gypsies living in the U.K. today. Undoubtedly, the Gypsies also intermarried with the Scots, the Welsh, and the Irish wanderers they fell in with on the road.

Today they can be encountered in London, Birmingham, Liverpool, Edinburgh and practically every other town in the British Isles. The majority are still constantly on the move, and since the war, less and less of their own volition. In the last decade or two, the authorities have passed various laws to encourage them to settle down on permanent camp sites, but this has met with opposition from local residents, who object to them as neighbors and to having their children sit beside them in class.

Following up a story in a London local newspaper about problems created by Gypsies occupying a site in the Holloway district, we took the opportunity to investigate the causes of the trouble for ourselves. It turned out that residents were fighting to have the Gypsies ejected from a site in Isledon Road, claiming that the lives of people living near the site had been seriously disrupted. "I was originally in favor of providing a well-supervized site, but after seeing the state of Isledon Road and the tens of thousands of pounds of damage, I am now withdrawing my support," a local councilor was quoted as saying. "The experiment has failed sadly. A lot of misery and anguish has been caused to residents." This camp was raised in the worst possible location, on rubble-strewn wasteground that could have been left from the wartime bombing. It stood near a public park and was typical of the sites set aside in response to the Caravan Site Act of 1968, which obliges local authorities to provide camping places for Gypsies. "When it comes to doing so," Rajko commented, "they usually allocate wasteground on industrial estates or in decaying urban neighborhoods, or next to railway lines, high overpasses, sewage treatment plants and landfills. And obviously, even here, families are not safe from eviction. The places where they had traditionally camped became out of bounds."

"There was no Gypsy problem until the Gypsy entered the 20th century," says Dennis Holmes, who is responsible for carrying out Birmingham's Gypsy eviction policy. In the past Gypsies camped in the countryside, mostly out of sight, like a part of nature. Moreover, they were useful as seasonal farm laborers – for example in the hop-fields of Kent. Now they have moved into cities, driven off the land by housing and other developments, the shrinking of the open spaces, and the mechanization of farming, and have become a nuisance to townsfolk.

As the three of us approached the entrance to the Isledon Road site, we were immediately spotted and set upon by a mob of the most unruly Gypsy children we had come across in our year-long journey – screaming and waving sticks at us menacingly, jumping on our backs, hitting and punching . . . Some started invading our pockets without any attempt to conceal their intention. Rajko tried to calm these wild and aggressive youngsters by speaking Romany, but they obviously did not understand it. Our every question met with the same standard response: "Why d'you want to know?" When we asked where they had come from, how long they had lived there, the children all answered in the way they had clearly been taught: "Why d'you want to know? What's it to you? Mind your own business. Leave us alone..." Their parents must have taught them to give no information to anyone, for strangers might trick them into admitting irregularities that could be used by the local people in their fight to drive the Gypsies away.

There was only one entrance into the Isledon Road camp – a narrow passage between two caravan trailers. Our first attempt to get in was thwarted by a snarling dog, whose chain was just the right length for him to guard the entrance and discourage intruders.

In view of the Gypsies' hostility towards outsiders, we gave up on the idea of photographing them, but I was set on entering the camp. A little while later, two youngish Gypsies got out of a fairly new Mercedes carrying large parcels and made for the entrance. Seeing my chance, I slipped in behind them, past the dog. I glanced around: some thirty trailers were parked haphazardly, and in front of three or four, women were cooking on primus stoves. Fortunately, the children we had first encountered had now vanished. A very powerfully built man emerged from a caravan and spoke to me rapidly in a variant of English I could scarcely understand. I immediately started telling him the story I had ready: "I'm looking for an Italian traveler, Antonio, who's living in a camp like yours in this area. I'm a relative of his." By this time a dozen or so other Gypsies had gathered round us. One asked how I had gotten in, and looked at the guard dog that was barking ferociously all the time. An elderly man answered my enquiry: "There are no Italian travelers here." I feigned surprise: "He should have arrived in London about a month ago! I'm also from Italy. Where are you from?" I asked casually. "We're Irish. We came here two months ago, and we haven't seen your Italian."

For them the conversation was over, and they started nudging me towards the exit. Between the caravans were chunks of rusty iron, broken furniture, old fridges and stoves – a sign that some of them collected scrap metal, as Gypsies do elsewhere in Europe. But these people, unlike their brethren in other European countries, had no desire for contact outside the group. Elsewhere, Gypsies would soon thaw out, show an interest in their visitor, offer him a seat, a drink, and be happy to chat, but no hospitality was offered here. In the center of London I felt less safe than in any Gypsy camp I had visited so far. On passing through the guarded entrance, with a feeling of relief I hurried to join my two friends waiting in the car. "Even a Gypsy guide wouldn't help here," Rajko said, "because these English and Irish Gypsies have no time for talk."

In the evening we visited an acquaintance of Rajko's, Tom Smith, who lives in a council house in the Camden Town area of London. He was alone at home: his wife was out working as an office cleaner. "Gypsy freedom is a thing of the past," Tom said. The first in his family to settle down, he sells second-hand furniture at local markets and enjoys a relatively comfortable life. "The days of traveling and camping are coming to an end. There are about 2,500 Gypsy caravans on authorized sites, but there are not enough of these, so illegal camping continues to create trouble and eyesores. People don't like it, and naturally there is a war, which the Gypsy is going to lose. Very soon we'll be gone. Then people will ask: 'Whatever happened to those nice Gypsies who used to sell pegs and tell fortunes?'"

EPILOGUE

Having spent a great deal of time with Gypsies all over the world in the past year or two, I felt that I had learned a tremendous amount. Visiting their settlements and traveling with them, I encountered an age-old way of life that, against all odds, has somehow survived into the 20th century, adapting itself perforce to alien cultures. On the garbage dumps of many countries another kind of life evolves parallel with ours, built up of the same dreams and wishes, loves, passions, hopes and despair, but on the very borderline of human existence.

Entering into this, even though only a spectator of sorts, I saw that it had taken me 50 years to finally rid myself of some misconceptions and prejudices acquired as a child. Any of my Montenegrin ancestors would have drawn a gun on someone for calling him a Gypsy. This name, in our part of the Balkans, was the greatest insult imaginable, implying that the person was a worthless human being, a thief and a liar, a cheat without any pride or dignity. If such an insult were uttered publicly, it often ended in a bloodied head or was paid for with one's life. Even the courts, when assessing the guilt of the accused, took into account such provocation as an extenuating circumstance.

After spending so much time with them, I realized that every Gypsy leads two lives, each with its own reality. The first is their Gypsy existence, their life on the road, in temporary camps, in the squalor of the "ghettos" on the fringe of "our" society; the second, the one they live in contact with us, Gadjas, during the time that they spend in our milieu, in passing only, for as long as it takes them to secure their existence. In order to live this life, they must learn our language, accept our religions and customs, serve us, amuse us . . . But how much do we really know about them?

In our work on this book, Zamur and I, and even Rajko, made many interesting discoveries about the Gypsies and gained a greater insight into their lives and ways. We hope our words and pictures have presented an objective view of this scattered and much persecuted people, and will help to destroy some of the widely-held prejudices which have caused the Gypsies so much suffering in the past.

N. B. T.

283

This map charts the approximate routes taken by the Gypsies on their long journey from Rajasthan in India to western Europe and thence the New World. The authors followed in their tracks many centuries later, visiting those countries in which the Gypsies stayed for longer periods of time on their travels and which still have a sizable Gypsy population. The only countries which the authors could not visit during their year-long journey, were Afghanistan and Iran, to which they were denied entry.

N

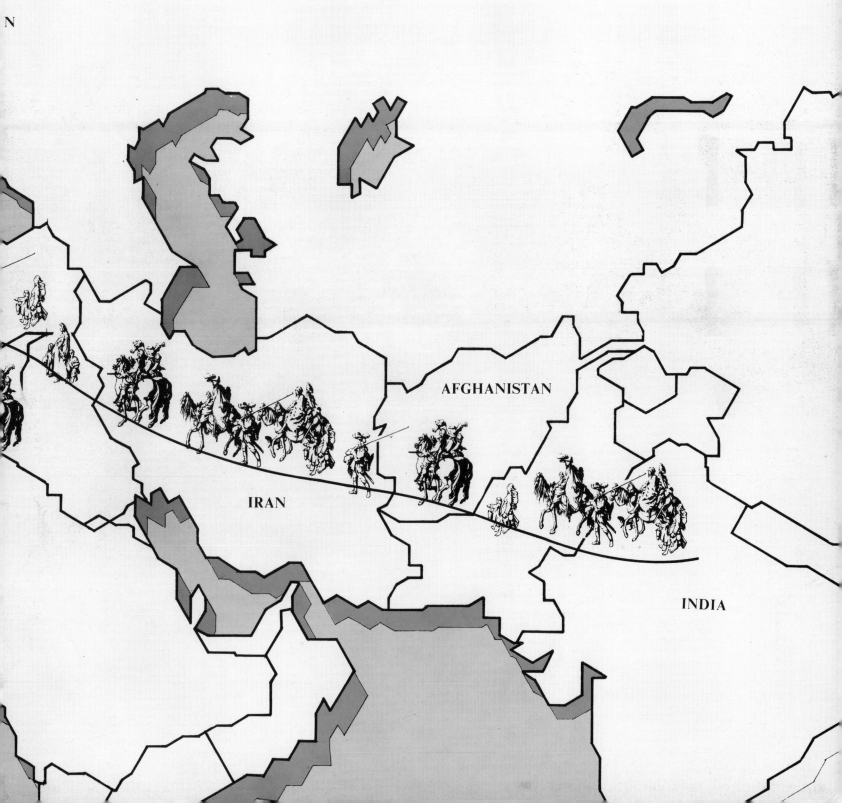

AFGHANISTAN

IRAN

INDIA

BIBLIOGRAPHY

of works mentioned in the book

J. Callot:
"Beggars: the blind man and his dog".
Etching.
(D. Ternois, "L'art de J. Callot",
Paris, 1962)

Chaman Lal: *Gypsies – Forgotten Children of India,* Ministry of Information of the Government of India, 1976

Donald Kenrick and Grattan Puxon: *The Destiny of Europe's Gypsies,* Chatto –Heinemann, London, 1972

Henrich Moritz Gottlieb Grellman: *Die Zigeuner – Ein Historischer Versuch über die Lebensart und Verfassung, Sitten und Schicksahle dieses Volks in Europa, nebst ihrem Ursprunge,* Dessau und Leipzig, 1783

Jawaharlal Nehru: *Discovery of India,* John Day Co., New York, 1960

F. N. Finck: *Die Sprache der Armenischen Zigeuner,* St Petersburg, 1907

Tatomir Vukanović: *Romi (Cigani) u Jugoslaviji,* Nova Jugoslavija, Vranje, 1983

J. Bompaire: *Actes de Xéropotamon, Archives de l'Athos,* III, 1964

D. Petrović: *Cigani u srednjevekovnom Dubrovniku,* Zbornik Filozofskog fakulteta, XIII-1, Belgrade, 1976

A. F. Pott: *Die Zigeuner in Europa und Asien,* Halle, 1844

F. Miklosich: *Uber die Mundarten und die Wanderungen Zigeuner Europas,* Vienna, 1872–1881

J. Callot:
"Beggars: beggar with crutches and bag".
Etching.
(D. Ternois, "L'art de J. Callot",
Paris, 1962)

INDEX

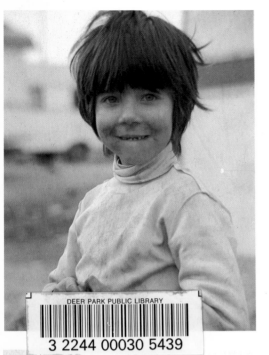